Living by Faith

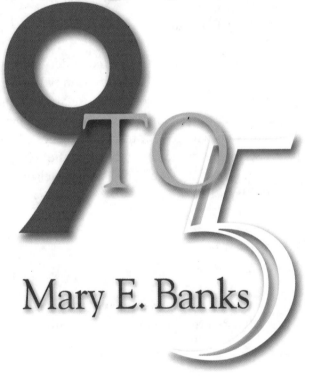

9 TO 5

Mary E. Banks

Evergreen
PRESS

ISBN 1-58169-216-1
For Worldwide Distribution
Printed in the U.S.A.

Evergreen Press
P.O. Box 191540 • Mobile, AL 36619
800-367-8203

TABLE OF CONTENTS

Dedication

To my husband and best friend, Melvin Kenneth,
a man of integrity and the absolute love of my life.

*Do you see a man who excels in his work? He will stand before
kings; he will not stand before unknown men.*
(Proverbs 22:29)

Honey, this one is for you...

Acknowledgments

As with any creative work, this book would not have been possible without the involvement of many wonderful people. My heartfelt thanks go to all of my colleagues, family and friends that took time to share their workplace stories with me. My heart was encouraged as I witnessed the power of God through both their failures and triumphs in the workplace, and I know many will be blessed as a result of their willingness to be transparent.

I greatly appreciate the support I always receive from my agent, Keith Carroll, who is my author coach and reinforces the importance of mentors in our lives. My thanks also go to the publishing team at Evergreen Press for having once again been amazing in catching the vision of my work and then assisting to make it even better.

But most importantly I want to thank Ken and Elise for always believing that what I write is something everyone needs to read and demonstrating that by cheering me on and encouraging me to run my race. I love you both and can't imagine my life without you.

Ultimately I want to thank my heavenly Father for sharing the story of Daniel with me. He must have known long ago that I would need an example like Daniel to teach me to live by faith 9 to 5.

PART ONE

Introduction

Everything I ever needed to know about surviving corporate America, I learned from the prophet Daniel. Unfortunately, I did not study his writings until I had made quite a few mistakes in the workplace. There are some things they just don't teach you in school—at least not in the schools I attended. As a result, I started my career believing that if I worked hard enough and kept my nose to the grindstone, I would find success. Boy was I naïve!

It makes me smile when I recall some of the mistakes I made, but they weren't so funny at the time. However, I've learned some important lessons throughout my long journey in the business world, lessons I wish I had known from the beginning. Many of these lessons came through trial and error, but overwhelmingly, one of the single best teachers that I have ever had to help me navigate through these seemingly shark invested waters has been Daniel. In fact, I secretly refer to him as the patron saint of the working person.

Throughout his story and the stories he shares about his friends, we see their faith tested time and again. They depend on a supernatural God to intercede on their behalf, and as a result, Daniel manages to survive what we commonly call the "rat race" of work. After all, who can forget the story of Daniel in the lion's den or the story of Daniel saving the day by interpreting the King's dream? And what about the fiery furnace encountered by Daniel's friends Shadrach, Meshach, and Abednego? These stories fascinate and intrigue me. So many important life lessons are contained in one very small book of the Bible.

What made Daniel unique is that he didn't just believe in God, he actually did what God said to do. As a result, we can all learn some timeless truths from Daniel's story. After all, if anyone had a tough working environment—it was Daniel. If anyone had backstabbing coworkers to deal with—it was Daniel. If anyone had a demanding boss—it was Daniel. Yet in spite of it all, I cannot think of anyone who modeled faith in the workplace in the way that Daniel did.

That's what this book is all about. Living your faith nine to five! In preparing to write this book, I talked with many working people—women and men of faith—just like you and me. I wanted to know what some of their most difficult challenges had been at work and how they had dealt with them. Consistently, the lessons I learned from Daniel resonated as truth as situation after situation was impacted by the simple precepts found in this ancient book of the Bible. I think it would be safe to say that these truths will stand the test of time.

After reading this book, you will know where talent and success truly originate, how to handle any work assignment, where to find the sponsorship that you need to be effective in any work you do, and how to deal with critics and competitors. Not only that, you will see the importance of saying and doing the right things no matter what consequences might occur and the value of viewing your work not as merely a job, but as an opportunity to serve others. Finally, you will learn the core principles of living your faith at work, and you will see, through the stories of Daniel and others, the challenges and the rewards of doing your work well.

Whether you are a person of faith who is about to begin a career, or a person that has been on the job for many years, it is not too late to learn what Daniel offers to teach you. You can walk in faith even in a seemingly hostile work environment. You can even work in what appears to be a fiery furnace and not have a hint of smoke on your clothes when it's all said and done. How? By applying the truth of God's Word as outlined in the book of Daniel.

The truth is that there really is a lion at work seeking whomever he can devour. If you have found yourself wondering whether you are just being paranoid or someone at work really is out to get you, then this book is for you! Each of us can get safely through the lion's den when we remember that God wants us to live our faith from nine to five.

Chapter One

Welcome to the Workplace!

Faith at Work Tip: Choose to have a great attitude at work—it is the one thing that is always on display.

Your attitude should be the kind that was shown us by Jesus Christ, who though He was God, did not demand and cling to His rights as God... (Philippians 2:5-6).

My knees were trembling just a little bit as I walked up to the podium. I was to give a presentation to many of the firm's officers on the state of the union for my department. Typically, I'm very good at extemporaneous speaking, but the Spirit had urged me to be better prepared this time, so I had actually practiced my presentation for a change. To be honest, I had practiced it many times, wanting to be sure that I was comfortable with the PowerPoint presentation and could remember by heart the statistics on some of the slides. *This should go well,* I thought to myself as I approached the front of the auditorium. *I am totally prepared!* Of course, I had this little speech going on inside of my head, trying to boost my confidence. As I turned to face my colleagues with a brilliant smile pasted on my face, the unthinkable happened—the technical assistant accidentally unplugged the computer containing my presentation, causing the overhead projector screen to go blank! This was not happening to me. I needed that presentation.

While remaining calm on the outside, I gently inquired as to how long it would take to reboot the computer and get my presentation back up on that screen. The assistant said with a slightly frightened look on her face, "About five minutes ma'am." At which point, I wanted to scream, "ARE YOU KIDDING? WHO HAS FIVE MINUTES?" There was an audience of 300 people waiting for me to get started. Instead of screaming, after gently urging the assistant to get the presentation back up and running as quickly as possible, I proceeded with my presentation as though nothing was amiss. Of course, I had to do it all from memory since there were no presentation notes to rely on, and I whispered a silent prayer, "Holy Spirit, please bring back to my memory everything that I prepared for this group. Please God, don't let me miss a beat and help me not to choke the assistant after I'm finished. Amen." Oddly enough, a peace settled over me as I heard myself going through the presentation. In fact, by the time the screen reappeared with my presentation and notes, I could tell I hadn't left out any important facts, and I was able to quickly move to the slide that I happened to be speaking on at the time.

Afterwards, my staff gave me a makeshift certificate they called the *Grace Under Fire Award*. I was delighted! As a leader, I was happy to have modeled grace to my team. I knew God's reflection appeared on that podium that day. Instead of becoming frustrated and even angry at the sudden turn of events, I was reminded by God that my attitude and my actions reflected on Him too. As I thought back on my preparation for that day, I had to smile because I remembered the Spirit gently nudging me to be better prepared than normal. Of course, he knew what was to come, and I've learned to listen to his soft, gentle leading. Having a positive attitude despite the circumstances is one lesson that continues to serve me well.

We all need a little help with finding a way through the maze that is known as the workplace. If you're like me, there are days when it is really hard to know which path would ultimately get you through the right corridor and which path would lead you to a dead end. Well, that's OK! Consider this to be your survival guide. Having gone through this particular maze a number of times, I've learned a few things that I believe will greatly benefit you. So let's start at the beginning....

In the Beginning...

Work was the first thing that our Creator assigned the first person to do. Adam was given the great responsibility to take authority over everything that had been created. Along with his wife Eve, he was the first worker. Back in their time, work was fun and new, creative and joyful. After all, no one had ever worked before, so there were no pre-conceived ideas about what work should be like. Many thousands of years have passed since then, and along with those years, generations have gained some experience in working: some positive, and some not so positive. Each generation passes on its ideas about how work should or shouldn't be done. That's great, but what happens if you were given a negative concept of work and your place in work? You could spend years trying to figure out how to be satisfied in your work or how to find purpose in it.

Thankfully, in Daniel, we have a great model of the proper approach to work. If you haven't read the story of Daniel in a while, now would be an excellent time to do so. When he entered the job market, it was the first true test of his character. He was surrounded by people who were very different from him; however, he quickly learned the customs, rules, and the culture of his new workplace. I'm sure he wanted, as everyone else did, to be successful. It was during my own faith journey that I first met Daniel. As I began my career, I struggled to determine my identity as a person of faith in a very strange land. I often looked to Daniel for instruction, encouragement, and truth. I wish I could say that I always took his advice, but that wouldn't be true. Instead, it was after getting knocked down a few times that I learned the value of reading God's Word and applying it. Much of this started when I first read the book of Daniel and began to see the similarities between his ancient Babylon and our modern day workplace. All the normal cast of characters and typical situations that you would see in any workplace were in Babylon, too—the difficult boss, the competitive colleagues, the tough assignments, the promotions and the demotions—all were there, and in the middle of the drama was Daniel.

Attitude and Faith

Despite the challenges and pressures that he faced everyday, there are two very important attributes of Daniel's character that will serve the working person well: Daniel had a great attitude and a great faith.

How can having a great attitude and great faith help us succeed in our jobs? Think of these two characteristics as being the glue that holds everything together and sets the person of faith apart from everyone else. In our culture, very few people have true and lasting faith in anything, and when such people are found, they stand out. Having a deep abiding faith in God, believing that He is real, believing that He is interested in our lives and desires a personal relationship with us is the type of faith we're talking about here. It's the type of faith that Daniel had, and it is what kept him going when the going got tough. It is this type of faith that causes a difference in one's attitude.

I have a friend who is a motivational speaker, and one of his favorite sayings is: "The only difference between a good day and a bad one is your attitude." How true this is. When you enter the workplace, your attitude will quickly become evident. If you believe that your work is something given to you by God that allows you an opportunity to serve others, you will approach your work with a positive attitude. On the other hand, if you see your work as being drudgery—something to be endured—your attitude will be less than positive, and it will show. How often I have met other believers in the workplace and thought the only way that I knew they were believers was the symbols or signs, such as *Believers Aren't Perfect, Just Forgiven*, on their desks. Their attitudes didn't reflect anything that suggested they believed in the God of the universe and that He had a great plan for their lives. Instead, they appeared to be barely hanging on and seemed to think that having the right religious symbols in their offices or Christian calendars on their desks would cause them to live victorious lives at work. I'm here to tell you—having enough religious signs of my own to know—that plaques don't add up to victory in the workplace. To the contrary, people see Christian symbols and then watch to see if there is any power exhibited in our lives to support the faith we profess.

The most powerful work tool you will ever have is the ability to project a positive attitude at work. By nature, people enjoy working around those who are optimistic, good humored, and positive. Even some of your grouchiest co-workers will gravitate towards a person with a great attitude because work is hard enough without having to be around grumpy, pessimistic people. In fact, people who are easy to get along with are twice as likely to get promoted as people who are not. Think about it. How many times have you seen people getting moved up in the company because they have a great relationship with the boss? You might have thought they were just being the proverbial "apple polishers," and it's possible that they were. However, it simply points out that which is obvious: People like to work with people whom they enjoy being around. A person with a great attitude is going to automatically have a few extra brownie points in the great interpersonal-skills category.

As a person of faith, you have so many reasons to come to work with a faith-filled attitude. First, your employer is not your source, God is. Your employer is merely being used as an instrument by God to bless your life. By being employed, you have the opportunity to earn a living, buy the things you need in life, contribute to your family's well being, and give to your church and community. Not only that, but you are also afforded the opportunity to learn some new skills and develop some existing ones. Second, working for a living can take you to an entirely new level of trusting in God. There might be no better way for God to teach you about true servanthood than for you to experience some complex work situations that can most assuredly test your faith. And most importantly, there is no better way to provide a witness for the joy you have as a believer than your being able to reflect that joy when you greet your co-workers each day at work.

Your workplace may be a great place to work, or it may have perpetual drama associated with it. No matter what your circumstances are, you can be certain that you are empowered to face your job with a victorious attitude if you start by preparing your heart before you arrive in the morning. Having a great attitude doesn't just happen. It takes work, and on some days a great attitude is easier to achieve than it is on other days. It begins by not allowing circumstances to dictate how you will behave and by choosing to respond to them in a positive way.

We are told in the Scriptures, "The weapons of our warfare are not carnal but mighty in God for pulling down strongholds, casting down arguments and every high thing that exalts itself against the knowledge of God, bringing every thought into captivity to the obedience of Christ" (2 Corinthians 10:4-5). Many times our bad attitudes are simply a high-minded way of saying that we know more than God does. When a situation that we don't understand occurs at work, it can affect our attitudes. If instead of recognizing that everything touching our lives must first be sifted through God's hands, we begin to take charge, then when things don't work out the way we had planned, our attitudes will take a downward spin. At such times, we must stop any "argument or high thing that exalts itself against the knowledge of God" (2 Corinthians 10:5). In other words, we need to confess what we know about Him and His character. What do we know?

- We know that He has a good plan for us (Jeremiah 29:11).
- We know that no matter how things look, He will work all our circumstances out for our good (Romans 8:28).
- We know that He loves us and is concerned about the things that concern us (1 Peter 5:7).

Because we know these things, we can go to our jobs each day with great attitudes and not allow circumstances to affect our behavior and defeat us before we even arrive. The following are three universal truths about our attitude.

1. *A great attitude starts in the mind.* If you think back to the last time you had a really bad attitude, you can more than likely trace it back to what you were thinking about before your attitude began to decline. You might believe that a person or a situation caused your attitude to become bad. But if you were to be honest with yourself, you would recognize that what you had thought about that person's motives or what you had thought about the situation was the real culprit. For example, if you believed that someone had sabotaged your work so that he/she would get promoted, you might start to think about that person in a negative way. Eventually, your thoughts toward that person would affect how you treated them, and ultimately, whenever you saw them, your attitude would become negative. On the other hand, if you were in that same situation and, instead of focusing on the person, you focused on the control God has in your life, your attitude would be completely different. In such a case, you would know that "no weapon formed against you will ever prosper" (Isaiah 54:17). And because you believed God's Word to be more powerful than the actions of that person, you would be inclined not to allow the person's actions to affect your attitude or your behavior.

2. *A great attitude is confirmed by our actions.* Once you have the Word of God in your heart and in your mind, it must reveal itself in how you

behave. In other words, you must do what you say you believe. What good is it to have many great Bible verses memorized if they are not evident in your life? If that is the case, you are living a life without power. And what good is that? One of the greatest mission fields a person of faith can have is their place of work. It is in this place where you can practice what you preach. You can love your neighbor as yourself, do good to those who contemptuously use you, and turn the other cheek. Oh, you didn't think you were actually going to have to do any of that stuff? Wrong! That is the reason we were placed exactly in the job we have today—to actively demonstrate the truth of God's Word through our obedient lives.

3. *A great attitude is cultivated through a mature spiritual life.* It is difficult to do good things and help others under your own power. Just as Daniel did, you must know God for yourself, and the only way you can know Him is to spend time with Him. For that reason, your personal quiet time with Him must be paramount in each day for you to experience success as a Christian in the workplace. Of course, you can experience some success by performing in your own strength, but this type of success will lack true meaning, and disillusionment will set in before you become aware of it. We will talk in later chapters about how God defines success, but suffice it to say that your work will take on new meaning and your attitude will be positively affected if you spend time each day quietly communing with God.

Spending time with God bolsters your faith. As you allow Him to minister the truth of His nature to your spirit, you will begin to trust Him more, and that will spill over into your thoughts, your attitude, and ultimately, your behavior. As we spend time with Him, we become more like Him. As our natures are changed, we begin to think differently and act differently. We become different people. Circumstances and situations that once pushed our buttons no longer have that power over us. People begin to notice a difference in the way we conduct ourselves. With our renewed lives, we will have an impact on others as we begin to work and live with purpose and meaning. And we will feel the deep satisfaction that comes from serving others.

During Daniel's time, he came to live and work in Babylon. This book will challenge you to define your own "Babylon." It is important to remember that Babylon is not a synonym for evil surroundings. Instead, I refer to the common, everyday workplace as Babylon. It is the place where we go to work, earn a living, and serve others. Babylon designates each of the places where we work during the years that we work, but the core concepts that govern how we work in Babylon will remain the same. Wherever your Babylon is, and at whatever stage of your career you happen to be, and whatever role you find yourself in— either an employee or an executive—as a person of faith, there are many life lessons for you to learn that will enhance your job performance. What is most important for you to know is that you can either create change in your Babylon or allow it to change you. The choice is yours. Will you be a person who works by faith from nine to five? Will you be one who allows His light to shine through you? Will you be one who chooses to make a difference? Will you be one who sees all of the possibilities ahead?

If everything within you says, "yes," then you are in for a great journey. Let it begin today.

Chapter Two

Decide in Your Heart

Faith at Work Tip: Decide in advance to live your faith at work.

Therefore Daniel purposed in his heart that he would not defile himself... (Daniel 1:8).

I first became acquainted with Daniel early on in my career. Even though Daniel died more than 600 years before the birth of Christ, and I was born 2000 years after Jesus' death, I still feel as though I have known Daniel for many years. I see him as being more than an ancient prophet from the Old Testament. I have come to know him as a trusted mentor, advisor, and friend. His words have spoken to me across the centuries separating our lives and revealed mysteries to me that I am certain would have gone unnoticed or would have been difficult for me to learn had I not experienced a bond with him.

You may wonder what a twenty-first century woman has in common with a sixth century Jewish man. It may not be obvious at first, but Daniel and I have much in common. In fact, as you get to know him better, you might find that you, too, have quite a bit in common with Daniel.

Daniel's Story

The story of Daniel is powerful. According to the Bible, Daniel was born around 620 B.C. and lived in the small country of Judah. In 605 B.C., King Nebuchadnezzar took him and other members of the royal family as captives to Babylon, where he remained for the rest of his days. What an amazing life he lived! Although he was taken away from everything that was familiar and important to him—family, friends, country, home, traditions—he still managed to keep what appeared to be most precious to him: his faith. From the moment you first encounter Daniel in the Bible, you understand that the young man was different, and you become engaged in his story due to the power of his magnificent personality.

Daniel had come from a country that had forgotten its roots. For centuries, the people of Israel had been obeying the laws given to them by Moses; however, due to the leadership of some of their kings, those years included periods when they lived in disobedience to God. During the reign of King Zedekiah, they became unfaithful to God and began to follow the pagan practices of the surrounding nations. Despite the many warnings given to them by the prophets, they refused to listen, and the king of Babylon was able to successfully conquer them. In fact, it is recorded in 2 Chronicles 36:17 that "God handed them all over to Nebuchadnezzar." Why did God allow this to happen? A glimpse of His reasons can be found in the Scriptures: "...so that they can learn how much better it is to serve me than to serve earthly rulers" (2 Chronicles 12:8).

We first read of Daniel and his friends Hananiah, Mishael, and Azariah, after they had been taken captive and transported to Babylon. It was common during that time for a king to take the most intelligent members from a territory he conquered and train them for service in the kingdom. It is noteworthy that Daniel and his friends were (more than likely) members of either the royal family or the nobility of Judah. Nebuchadnezzar believed that due to their status within Judah, they could deter a rebellion from the other Jewish captives who were in Babylon.

Because we know the purposes for which they were selected, we also know some important information about Daniel and his friends. They would have been chosen at a young age because it was believed that youths were more teachable and more willing to learn than were adults. Those selected were required to be in good health and have a pleasing appearance. A high level of intelligence was also a criterion since they would ultimately serve as advisers to the king. All those who were allowed to be in the presence of the king had to possess certain social skills, so we know that Daniel and his friends either had the skills or exhibited the ability to learn the skills that were required for serving in the royal court. It was customary for the training to last for three years.

Daniel and his friends not only received a privileged education but were also to receive a privileged diet. They were to be fed from the king's table, which was the best food in the land. Daniel's name and the names of all of his friends were changed. "Daniel," which in Hebrew means "God is my judge," was changed to Belteshazzar, which was the name of a pagan god and meant "protect his life." His friend Hananiah was renamed Shadrach, Mishael's name became Meshach, and Azariah became known as Abednego. Their Hebrew names were references to God, whereas the Babylonian names they were given referred to a pagan deity. Despite the attempt by their captors to make them lose their identity, the young men developed a resolve to remain steadfast in their faith in God.

The first test of Daniel's faith came when he was told his diet would consist of the foods that were served at the royal court. This meant he would have to eat foods that were forbidden by the Jewish dietary laws. For him to refuse the royal diet would have been a great insult to the king and could have resulted in Daniel's being immediately executed. However, in spite of this, Daniel had made up his mind that he was not going to defile himself and risk displeasing God by eating the royal food. Daniel had a plan. He decided to ask one of the guards for permission to eat an alternative diet, one that would not be in violation of his religious beliefs. Initially, the guard feared that doing so would cause Daniel and the others to appear to be unhealthy, which would result in the loss of his job. So Daniel suggested there be a trial alternative diet for ten days, after which the guard would judge whether or not the new diet had harmed their physical condition.

The Old Testament account of this story indicates that God caused the guard to have a favorable attitude toward Daniel, and as a result, he agreed to Daniel's request. After being on the diet for ten days, Daniel and his friends looked healthier and better nourished than the young men who had been eating the food assigned by the king! As a result, the guard allowed them to continue eating the diet Daniel had chosen in obedience to God.

Lesson 1: You must first be determined to live your faith at work!

Before Daniel ever began his new job—while he was still in training—he made a decision. He purposed in his heart that he was going to live his faith at work, which means he made a decision and re-solved to stick with it. He did so because he had committed to living by faith, regardless of the circumstances. Daniel had already seen the consequences of abandoning one's faith. After all, he was a captive be-cause his community, the people he knew and loved, had decided to follow their own way instead of God's way. As a result, he and his friends had been among the few survivors of a hostile take-over and were now captives being prepared to work on the king's staff. He had experienced the disaster of not walking in faith and had decided that his life would be different. He wanted to be one who lived by faith and who trusted God to be true to His Word. Because he knew that God had promised in 2 Chronicles 7:14, "If my people who are called by my name will humble themselves and pray and seek my face and turn from their wicked ways, I will hear from heaven and will forgive their sins and heal their land."

What were some of the work situations that could have tempted Daniel to abandon his faith? They were the same situations that typi-cally face us every day. No person of faith goes to work with the thought: *Today, I'm not going to demonstrate my faith in God.* Instead, a pattern of factors typically exists in our interactions with others or in certain situ-ations or events that causes us to begin to veer off the path of faith. These factors typically fall into four different categories:

1. **Peer pressure**—That subtle internal pressure that causes us to want to do what others are doing, either to fit in with the crowd, or at minimum, to be accepted by our peers

2. **Ambition**—While not a bad thing in and of itself, if left uncon-trolled (without boundaries), it can affect our ability to follow God's leadership in our lives

3. **Anonymity**—The mistaken sense that no one will know that we have violated a core principle of our faith

4. **Doubt**—That secret belief that God isn't truly able to protect us in any situation

Now let's look at a contemporary example of how these factors can intermingle in today's workplace. This story is about three men. All of them worked for the same company, and all of them had senior level jobs that paid very well. Joe, who was one of the three men, was a Christian—or at least that is how he described himself. Joe was the finance administrator on his church's board and attended church every Sunday. At work, he was an exceptional performer and always worked hard to please his customers and make money for his firm. In fact, he was a managing director in his department.

But Joe had a secret. Joe and two of his friends had habits of sending one another friendly e-mails. Some of the e-mails contained silly stories and jokes, while others contained pictures of women and men in various stages of undress, performing different sexual acts. Joe and his friends got a big kick out of sharing these pictures among themselves and with their customers. After all, they were all consenting adults. Who were they hurting? The thought of what he was doing began to nag at Joe deep inside. He knew it was against company policy to use the company's computer system to transmit pornographic material, so he decided to stop sending the pictures. However, despite the fact that he was the manager, he didn't discourage his friends from sending pictures to him. After all, he didn't want to appear to be a stick-in-the-mud or a party-pooper. Instead, he told them to be careful that they not send the pictures to anyone who might be offended by them. This worked fairly well for about a year. Joe wasn't sending any pictures, but he was still enjoying receiving them from his friends.

One day, the company audited the e-mail system and discovered what Joe and his friends had been doing. All three of them were fired! Joe was devastated. After all, he was on his church's board. What would he do if the word got out that he had been fired for allowing pornography to be viewed in his department?

Where did Joe go wrong? Initially, Joe succumbed to peer pressure. He participated in transmitting inappropriate emails so that he would be accepted as one of the guys. But eventually, something deep inside began to speak to him and tell him that what he was doing was wrong. That something was God's still, small voice. It was an opportunity for Joe to go to God and confess that he had sinned. He could then have asked God for direction in correcting the wrong example that he had set in his office.

But that isn't what he did. Instead, he thought that since his actions were not known outside of the company, he could just stop sending the e-mails and everything would be fine. In other words, he concentrated on what everyone else would think about his actions and not on what God would think. Joe was focused on getting ahead, and he believed that he would appear odd to his colleagues and customers if he began preaching about the wrong he had done by sending the pictures. And besides, Joe seriously doubted that God could protect him in such a situation. Although Joe viewed himself as a person of faith, his actions provided a startling contrast to what he claimed to be.

Is Joe's story any different than Daniel's? Actually, it is a similar situation, but the stories have different outcomes. Think about how easy it would have been for Daniel and his friends to succumb to peer pressure. After all, everyone was eating the king's diet, and there certainly was no way that their family or friends would ever find out they had been eating forbidden foods. Their parents and everyone else they knew were hundreds of miles away. Furthermore, by adhering to their odd dietary customs, they could have easily been viewed as too odd to ever be considered for advancement and might have sacrificed any opportunity for a promotion in the king's court. And finally, it would have been easy for them to become discouraged and think that since God didn't protect them from being taken captive, he would not come through for them regarding that. Even so, they didn't react in any of those ways.

How did Daniel respond to the seductive influences of peer pressure, ambition, anonymity, and doubt? Before he arrived at work that morning, he had made up his mind to walk in faith. He started each day with a heart purposed to do what he knew would please God.

Now, before we decide that we could never do what poor Joe did, let's ask ourselves these questions:

- Am I known to criticize my boss in an unkind manner?
- Do I gossip about others with my co-workers?
- Do I feel jealous when someone else gets the promotion that I believe should have been mine?
- Have I lied about being sick, simply to avoid going to work?
- Do I take company supplies that don't belong to me?

Some of you may be able to truthfully answer "no" to all of those questions, but I think you know the point that is being made here. We all could make up a list of examples of times when we could have done a much better job of living out our faith at work. So how do we learn to emulate Daniel's example?

Start by realizing that your life may be the only "Bible" some people ever read and that your words may be the only sermon that someone at work ever hears. Before you leave the house, or before you enter your place of work, pray and ask God to:

1. Guard your mind and keep you from thinking about anything that does not edify God
2. Guard your actions and keep you from doing anything that would displease God and would hurt others
3. Guard your tongue and keep you from saying anything that doesn't edify God or help others

Lesson 2: Guard your mind.
Our actions and words start first in our mind. Jesus described it this way,

> It is the thought-life that defiles you. For from within, out of a person's heart, come evil thoughts, sexual immorality, theft, murder, adultery, greed, wickedness, deceit, eagerness for lustful pleasure, envy, slander, pride, and foolishness. All these vile things come from within; they are what defile you and make you unacceptable to God (Mark 7:20-23).

Jesus was basically saying that we should think about what we are thinking about. If we are thinking negative thoughts about others, our words and actions will soon follow along that path. However, if we are thinking affirming thoughts about others, our words and actions will follow that path. We need God's help to do this each day.

Lesson 3: Guard your actions.
If we say that we are people of faith, then we must be people concerned about our actions and what our actions say about us. In the Bible, James explains it this way,

...what's the use of saying you have faith if you don't prove it by your actions? It isn't enough just to have faith. Faith that doesn't show itself by good deeds is no faith at all—it is dead and useless...our ancestor Abraham was declared right with God because of what he did when he offered his son Isaac on the altar...You see, he was trusting God so much that he was willing to do whatever God told him to do. His faith was made complete by what he did—by his actions (James 2:14-22).

When we go to work, our actions should be a reflection of our faith. If we believe that God is who he says he is, then he is able to sustain us through any situation we will face, and our actions should exhibit our confidence in Him.

Lesson 4: Guard your tongue.
This is not an easy task, and it requires great discipline on our part and supernatural intervention on God's part. The Scriptures say, "...those who control their tongues can also control themselves in every other way" (James 3:2). Even though our tongues are small, they can do enormous damage. The power of life and death is in the tongue. We can speak blessings into the lives of others or we can speak curses. Don't believe the old adage "sticks and stones may break my bones but words will never hurt me." It is not true! Our words can have a devastating effect on others. They can also be used to encourage and uplift someone during a time of emotional need. We should never underestimate the power of our tongue.

So, what does this all mean? Tell God that you are ready to do battle! Tell him you are ready to go to the M.A.T. to live your faith and that you need His help. This is what Daniel learned to do. It is what kept him from violating the beliefs that he held dear. He had determined in his heart and had resolved to do whatever it would take to walk in faith. With God's help, we can too! Because at the end of the day, it comes down to the one key question that God is asking to all of us: What have you purposed in your heart?

Chapter Three

Learn the Culture

Faith at Work Tip: Serve others by learning to 'speak their language'

Therefore let us pursue the things which make for peace and the things by which one may edify another (Romans 14:19).

Many years ago, in the dawn of my career, I went to work for a very distinguished firm. I had come from a company that had very few unspoken rules and they had been pretty laid back. So when I started my new job at this firm, I had no notion of what was expected of me other than what was listed on the job description that had been given to me prior to my starting. To celebrate my new job, I bought a new pair of red shoes to wear on my first day. They were fabulous! The heels were tall and spiky, and the toes on the shoes had points as sharp as knives. The three-and-a-half inch heels gave me added height, and I felt empowered by those shoes.

I couldn't wait for the first day of work, so that I could show off those red shoes. They were bright and went very well with the flashy dress I had chosen to set them off perfectly. When I arrived for new hire orientation at my office, I noticed immediately that something was amiss. I instantly sensed that the other people in the room didn't quite get how truly wonderful my new shoes were. In fact, they seemed to be looking at me with a sense of horror, and as I looked back at them, I realized there were absolutely no bright colors in the room. Everyone there had on either a black or navy blue business suit. As a result, my red shoes and my flashy dress stuck out like a sore thumb. I was mortified!

Did I miss the memo about no red shoes? Certainly not! What I was unfamiliar with was the concept of workplace culture. Clearly, this was a company that wanted to present itself as conservative, serious, and business-like. It had interpreted these qualities into every fabric of the organization, including the mode of dressing. I later found that there was no dress code—nothing stated that employees were to wear black or navy blue suits. Instead, everyone there knew that conservative business attire meant black or navy blue suits because that was a part of the culture of the firm.

So, what is corporate culture, and why is understanding it important to the person of faith? Culture is something we know when we see it, but it is difficult to define. Imagine a fish trying to define the water he swims in. A fish is so much a part of his environment that he doesn't really notice it, but he would certainly miss it if it were suddenly to be gone. The same is true about culture in a business setting. Each company has its own beliefs, expectations, values, and traditions that set the unwritten norms. Corporate culture can help all members of an organization work together toward common goals. To a person of faith who has been called to do her job excellently, but who also sees it as an opportunity to serve God, understanding the culture where she works and working within it can ultimately lead her to be a more effective witness for the faith centered life.

A Lesson From Daniel

When Daniel first arrived at his new job as adviser to the king in Babylon, he was in a totally foreign culture. He learned all that he could learn about the new culture so that he would be able to do an excellent job at work. He was wise enough to realize a truth that the Apostle Paul spoke many centuries later.

> *I have become a servant of everyone so that I can bring them to Christ...when I am with the Gentiles who do not have the Jewish law; I fit in with them as much as I can. In this way, I gain their confidence and bring them to Christ. But I do not discard the law of God; I obey the law of Christ* (I Corinthians 9:19-21).

Daniel knew that learning the culture would not make him disloyal to God. It would not be in violation of God's commands, but instead it would cause him to be more effective in his work, and therefore, a better example of the excellence that God brings out in his people. As a result, he learned about the corporate culture, achieved excellence in his work, served the king faithfully, prayed for God's guidance, and maintained his integrity.

Being in Babylon Without Becoming a Babylonian

Have you ever worked at a place where everyone was consumed with the notion of getting ahead, and before you realized it, you began to behave exactly the way everyone else was behaving? In Babylon, during the biblical days, the people's mentality was to think: I am, and there is no one else besides me (Isaiah 47:8, 10).

How similar to then, things are today. We all work among people who have the mentality that no one is more important than they are, and that their needs must be met no matter who gets hurt in the process. A common expression used at work is "What's in it for me?" The biggest challenge we face when working in any environment is to not allow the environment to define us. It's OK for us to want to succeed, but our methods for achieving success should always have a biblical perspective, and not be simply ones that we adopt from our surroundings. You can actually be in Babylon without becoming a Babylonian! One way to do so is to learn the corporate culture of your company and set boundaries that define what will set you apart from the others who work there.

Assessing the Culture

Assessing the corporate culture of a company is critical to understanding what is considered acceptable and what is not acceptable at that company. When assessing your company's corporate culture, you should consider how the staff interact with others, how the staff dress, what is the general atmosphere of the company, and how the company is portrayed by former employees and in the news. How will knowing this help you? This can provide you with useful information about how a public demonstration of faith will be received. For example, is it acceptable to have scriptural quotes on the signature line of your e-mail? Can you display religious symbols in your work area? Will management allow a Bible study group to meet in one of the company meeting rooms? These are all questions that speak directly to the issue of your company's culture.

Remember, God wants us to be respectful of the authority figures that He has placed in our lives. Sometimes we mistakenly think that it is our job to defend God at work; He is perfectly capable of defending Himself. The culture in which we work may have very different rules about the way faith is practiced in the workplace. My friend June learned this the hard way.

June worked at a local retail store, selling shoes. She was a good employee and typically met her sales goals. It was not unusual to hear June talking about God throughout the workday. Many times she talked with her customers about Him and asked them if they knew Jesus. She also told them her personal testimony and encouraged them to get saved.

One day, June had a customer that really hated the fact that she was talking to him about God, and he told her as much. June was not deterred. She proceeded to tell her customer that his attitude was bad because he needed God in his life. An argument ensued, and the customer asked to see the manager. When the manager arrived, the customer complained loudly that he hadn't come into the store to hear June preach at him. He simply wanted to buy a pair of shoes. After apologizing to the customer and completing the sale, the manager turned to June and told her she had to stop evangelizing at work. June took great offense to this request because she thought it impeded her religious freedom. Besides, she believed that it would be disloyal to God for her to keep her mouth closed when so many people were lost and needed to know about him.

After the incident, June decided that she was going to continue to talk to her customers about God despite the fact that her manager had told her not to do so. And so she did. Shortly after she made that decision, another customer complained about June's evangelizing. This time, she was given a written warning by her manager and was told that if she did not stop evangelizing at work, she would be dismissed from the company. June was appalled at the warning. She fully expected God to intercede because she believed that He was on her side.

June continued as though she had not received the warning and made a point to ask the very next customer if they knew Jesus. The customer was greatly offended by the question and reported June to the manager. After a brief investigation into the matter, June was fired. She couldn't believe it! How could God possibly allow her to get fired simply because she was trying to spread the word about Him?

How could He indeed? Living our faith at work doesn't give us the license to ignore some basic principles that God has put in place to maintain order and discipline in our lives. It's easy to see that June was more interested in acting on her desire to see those around her become saved than she was interested in following God's leading concerning His work and asking Him for the appropriate opportunities to share her faith. Who can say whether or not June would have been used to paint a beautiful picture of faith in the life of her manager had he observed her being respectful of his request that she not evangelize in the workplace. Instead, it's highly possible that he was left with the impression that God's people don't do the work they are paid to do and spend their time annoying others. Surely, this is not the example that people of faith want to give the world.

Considering this, the best time to assess the culture of the workplace may be before you have even started your job. If you are fortunate to have the opportunity to do this in advance, begin talking to people who already work there. Ask them about the culture of the company. Research the company at the library or on the Internet by reading recent articles about the company or reviewing their annual report. This can give you glimpses into what the company is all about. It can also help you decide whether or not it is a culture that is suitable for you. If practicing your faith in a very public way is critical to your being happy at work, wouldn't it be best for you to know and understand the perspective the company has on the issue before you accept a position with them?

On the other hand, what if you are already working for a company with a culture that would make it next to impossible for you to even speak God's name in the workplace? You have two possible alternatives: you can quit, or you can decide to let God be your God. What I mean is that if God has planted you there, then He is fully capable of showing you how to demonstrate your faith in a manner that doesn't violate the workplace rules, but allows others to see Him in you.

If we are truly to be useful to God in the workplace, we must carefully assess our present situation at work and development awareness to the opportunities that surface, allowing us to share our faith with others. That is what finding the balance means. The opportunities will be different in every workplace because corporate cultural environments differ from one another. However, learning to successfully model your faith through your actions rather than merely by what you say will have a substantial impact on others. The old adage, "Actions speak louder than words," is true in this case. Your coworkers will watch the life that you live and believe it much more than they will hear or believe the words that you say.

Why Knowing the Culture Is So Important

Clearly assessing a company's culture will help you understand how best to navigate it. But there is another reason to really excel in this area. Once you have a thorough knowledge of your company's culture and learn to follow the unspoken rules, you will begin to gain credibility with those you most want to influence. For example, let's imagine you work in a place where the office hours are from 8:00 a.m. to 5:00 p.m., however, the unspoken rule is that you really need to stay until 6:00 p.m. to be considered a hard worker. You might have even noticed on the few occasions when you remained past 5:00 p.m. that not much work was really getting done. In fact, it might have appeared that people were doing more socializing than work. You might have wondered why you should hang around if people are just standing around talking. You have better things to do at home! What's really going on here? This is where being able to effectively assess your workplace cultural norms becomes critical. Why are people remaining after 5:00 p.m.?

1. They notice that those who get promoted work later than others.
2. The boss tends to penalize those who do not.
3. People are using that time after hours to get to know one another better—to develop a stronger team

If you observed that after hours your co-workers were spending more time socializing than working, then you would probably conclude that number three is the answer. If that were the case, you may decide to occasionally remain after hours to learn more about your colleagues and to develop rapport with them. You would gain credibility by showing an active interest in them and by being willing to invest some of your own time in getting to know them better.

On the other hand, using that same example, what if you found that people were really working hard after hours because there was a deadline that had to be met in their business unit while your business unit was having a slow period? Again, if you were to assess the situation and discover that to be the case, you may decide in that situation to offer assistance (if you have the capability to be of help). If you were to do so, you would gain credibility by others realizing that you know how hard they are working and by being willing to sacrifice some of your time to help them. And what a great way to demonstrate your faith! Remember, others will give more weight to your actions than they will to what you have to say. That is why knowing your company's culture is so important.

What To Do When the Culture Doesn't Fit

What if you find that the place where you work has a culture that is simply intolerable? That is the situation in which Millie found herself. She had joined a company as the new training manager and had been told that the company had a serious problem with nepotism stemming from the fact that the president of the company hired relatives who were not qualified for the jobs they filled. The culture of the company promoted an environment that was not based on meritocracy, but on family relationships. This didn't discourage Millie, despite the fact that she soon learned that she would be managing the president's brother-in-law. She believed that if she had any problems with the brother-in-law, she would need to document her conversations and actions well to avoid any misunderstandings.

What Millie did not count on was the fact that the president's brother-in-law believed himself to be highly talented even though he had been unsuccessful in various positions within the company. His latest passion was to be a trainer, despite the fact that he had no prior experience, no related education, and basically no natural talent for the job. Millie coached him on a development plan that included an opportunity for him to take training seminars to begin building his knowledge on the training basics.

Shortly thereafter, problems begin to surface because the president's brother-in-law was unaccustomed to being held to a performance standard. Due to the firm's practice of hiring the president's relatives, a culture had evolved to the point where no one attempted to hold his relatives accountable; all were afraid of offending the president. That is, until Millie came along. She believed that it wasn't fair to hold her other staff members to a high standard of performance and not require the same of the brother-in-law. One day, to her dismay, she was called into the president's office to be severely scolded for her treatment of his brother-in-law. She learned that the president had been told many untruthful things concerning her dealings with him. Since she had kept her own manager apprised of all of her actions concerning the brother-in-law, she was able to request that her manager join the meeting, and he was able to refute what the president had been told.

After this incident, it became clear to Millie that the cultural environment did not fit what she believed to be critically important to any workplace in which she was to remain. She knew that despite the fact she had been successful in overcoming this particular situation with the brother-in-law, nepotism would continue to be a problem that would result in no accountability for any relative of the president. As a result, she made a decision to resign her position and trust God to provide her with another job. She felt a calm peace about the decision, despite having no other job. A remarkable thing occurred. On the very day that she resigned, her former employer contacted her and offered her a position with a higher salary than what she had formerly been making! That was exactly the confirmation she needed to know that her decision was indeed the right one. She had learned an important lesson— when God puts you in a place, stand still until He tells you to move, including remaining faithful to a task that you have been assigned. Once your task is completed, God will let you know when it is time to move on.

Finding the Balance

In all things there must be a balance. There is a time to speak up and a time to be quiet. So it is when you have learned to understand the culture of the place where you work. You will find there will be times when you may openly speak about your faith and other times when you must silently model it. One way is not better than the other; they are just different. When you are being guided by the spirit of God, either approach will be effective in the circumstances that you find you must adjust to. The apostle Paul said it best about this, "you must accept whatever situation the Lord has put you in, and continue on as you were when God first called you" (I Corinthians 7: 17). This simply means that you can do God's work and demonstrate your faith anywhere, but you must first ask God for the wisdom to know the right approach for the work environment and the culture in which He has placed you.

Chapter Four

Understand the Diversity

Faith at Work Tip: You will recognize true believers by the way they love others

Beloved, let us love one another, for love is of God; and everyone who loves is born of God and knows God. He who does not love does not know God, for God is love (1 John 4:7-8).

Diversity, diversity, diversity! It seems that the work "hot-button" for the twenty-first century is diversity in the workplace. It is important to understand the distinctions of your place of work because you are going to be working with many different types of people, and you will be challenged to get along with those who may be very different from you. Diversity in a typical workplace is defined as differences in gender, race, color, nationality, religion, and culture. Indeed, we can describe diversity in this manner and be politically correct. But for the believer in Christ, it is important to recognize another diversity component—how God is viewed in the workplace. The true disciple of Christ should know that living by faith means different things to different people.

This simply means that there are very few people who are actually living examples of their faith in God. If you are a person of faith, you need to know one thing about your workplace—you are probably in the minority. There is also diversity among those who call themselves people of faith, and it is easy to recognize once you stop assuming that all people of faith are the same. Most of the people we work with will fall into one of four categories: the atheist, the spiritual, the religious, and the true disciple.

The Atheist

This group is easiest to recognize because people who would describe themselves in this way basically don't believe that God exists. To them, faith in God is not a factor for consideration, and it is viewed as a useless exercise. The atheistic doctrine, simply stated, is that there is no deity.

The Spiritual

Those who would be considered spiritual typically have some sense of God's existence; they're just not sure exactly who or what He is, and some have difficulty understanding exactly where He is. To them, faith may be a belief in "the god in you," or it may be simply a belief in themselves. They may view the spirit as a prime element of reality and may indeed have a sensitivity or attachment to religious values. However, they do not usually identify with one particular deity and may be accepting of many different deities.

The Religious

People who are described as religious generally have some formal religion that they are attached to and doctrine were brought up to believe. The members of this group may be the ones who are most often confused with true disciples of Christ. This confusion exists because many of them call themselves Christians. Yet, it takes little time to determine that they have no relationship with Christ, and therefore, are not truly His followers. Their faith usually is based mainly on a set of moral rules that may be biblically based, but it is not based on a true encounter with the risen Savior. They clearly relate to, and accept the ultimate reality of God, but may accept many different ways of forming a meaningful relationship with him.

The True Disciple

Finally, there is the true follower, or disciple, of Christ. They are the ones who professes belief in the teachings of Jesus Christ and demonstrate through their actions that they have personal relationships with Christ and have made Him Lord and Savior of their lives. Although not perfect, they have made it the mission of their lives to exhibit the characteristics of Christ through their behaviors, their thinking, and their words in whatever circumstances they are in. To them, faith is the only means by which they can please God, and they view their lives and work as being faith in action.

With so much diversity among those who may view themselves as people of faith, one begins to wonder what a true person of faith looks like. The real essence of the people you may encounter at work will demonstrate the truth of their discipleship in Christ.

Always Look for the Fruit!

If you want to know what type of tree there is in a garden, what would be the first clue? If you said, "examine the fruit," you would be right. An apple tree is going to produce only apples. You will never see an orange on an apple tree. Likewise, you will never see an apple on an orange tree. Although people are not always as consistent as trees, the core of a person can be evaluated over time. By observing a person over an extended period of time, you should be able to see the fruit from their lives, and it will give witness to what they believe and who they believe in.

So what fruit are you exhibiting, person of faith? Would someone observing your life be able to tell what you believe in and to whom you belong? Are you showing through your actions the fruit that comes from only the Spirit of God? Love, joy, peace, patience, kindness, goodness, faithfulness, gentleness, and self-control are the fruits that a person who is controlled by God's spirit will demonstrate on a consistent basis (Galatians 5:22-23). It is not an easy task in the modern day workplace as so many try in their own strength to appear as apple trees when they are really orange trees. However, the true fruit always shows itself eventually, and it becomes increasingly obvious who is merely talking the talk and not walking the walk. If we are being led by God in our everyday lives, then others should never see us exhibiting the following behaviors:

- Constantly talking about what everyone else is doing wrong but never examining areas in our life that could use refinement
- Often reading our Bibles but seldom being observed actually doing anything it says
- Confessing our love for God but not loving some other people

- Faithfully attending religious services but typically not being known to apply any of the principles of our faith in our day-to-day lives
- Living in such a way that if we admitted to being a person of faith, the reaction of others would be great surprise

Do some of these items describe you? If the answer to that question is "yes," then begin to consider again the fruit that you want to demonstrate and ask God to begin any changes He needs to make in you. Diversity of this nature in the workplace matters a lot. Many people at work will judge you based on assumptions they have about others who may use the same title to describe a very different faith. For example, you may find many who identify themselves as Christians but who may really be Christians in name only. Consequently, your co-workers may initially judge you based on their prior experiences with those who falsely identified themselves by the same name. Some of their preconceived notions may be that you are judgmental, non-inclusive, hypocritical, and legalistic. As a result, you may not be received with open arms when it is discovered that you are a person of faith.

It is just as it was in Daniel's day. He, too, was surrounded by co-workers who had spiritual beliefs that were different from his. In his day, they were called magicians, enchanters, sorcerers, and astrologers, and they all believed that they had true wisdom and knowledge from the gods. Daniel stood out because he believed in the Most High God, and it was his faith that governed his actions at work and in his daily activities. Instead of allowing their differences to create barriers, Daniel learned to embrace the differences between him and those he worked with to demonstrate the faithfulness of his God. He didn't condemn others for their beliefs even when he didn't agree with them. Instead, he used his own faith to demonstrate again and again the love that God gave him for others.

I once read a story that clearly demonstrated the difference between talking about faith and living it. During World War II there was a soldier at boot camp in basic training. He shared the barracks with many other soldiers who were also being trained. This soldier was known for his deep faith in God and was often seen reading his Bible or praying by the side of his bed before the lights went out in the barracks.

For some reason, this was very irritating to one of the other soldiers, and he frequently taunted him—swearing and saying there was no God—as the Christian knelt in prayer. But this never distracted the young soldier, and he continued with his routine every night.

One evening, the angry soldier came in from guard duty and saw his fellow soldier praying. This made him so mad that he took off one of his muddy boots and threw it at the praying soldier. The boot hit the side of the soldier's head leaving a trail of mud on the side of his face, but he never looked up. Instead, he continued to pray. This made the soldier even madder, so he removed his other muddy boot and threw it as well at the praying soldier. There was no response! The soldier continued to pray. Finally, in frustration, the angry soldier shook his head in disgust, undressed, and went to bed.

The next morning when he awakened, sitting on the floor next to his bed, were his boots. But they were no longer caked with mud as they had been the previous night. They had been cleaned and polished, and there was no indication that they had ever been in the mud. The sight of his freshly polished boots so touched the heart of the soldier that he broke down and wept due to the kindness shown to him. He went immediately to find the praying soldier because he wanted to know more about the God whom he served.

What a marvelous example of faith in action! The praying soldier exhibited his faith in God by not only turning the other cheek to someone who had treated him cruelly but also blessing him. We will encounter many opportunities in the workplace to exhibit the same type of faith and to demonstrate the difference that Christ makes in our lives. Be cognizant that these are opportunities to demonstrate the heart of Christ towards your co-workers. Show them what Christ-like behavior really looks like.

You can also set an example by respecting the diversity of thought that exists between people that come from different religious backgrounds. Even though you and your co-workers may not agree on accepted universal truths, you can handle these varied points of view respectfully without sacrificing your own belief system. Remember, the God of the universe does not need you to defend Him. He is capable of handling His own defense. He does require you to walk in love and to share His attributes of demonstrating as often as possible His heart for people and the difference having a personal relationship with Him has made in your life. This approach will create acceptance of you and your faith—more so than having a hundred heated arguments about whether or not God exists or whether or not Jesus was actually God. It is the work of the Holy Spirit to change the hearts of people. This frees you to go to your workplace without having the extra assignment of changing people's lives.

So how can you show respect when attempting to demonstrate your faith around someone whose faith is in direct contradiction to your own? The answer is—very thoughtfully and prayerfully. Here are a few guidelines that may be helpful:

1. **Keep it simple**—let people know who you really are by being authentic. Don't try to impress them with your doctrinal knowledge or exhibit a "holier than thou" attitude. Remember always that you were saved by grace through no effort of your own, and this will keep you humble and useful to God as you encounter others.

2. **Seek to understand**—attempt to understand the spiritual backgrounds of your co-workers. When conversations naturally lend themselves to this type discussion, seek to learn why they believe the way they do. This may provide an opportunity for you to share your faith as well.

3. **Be consistent**—just because you are tolerant of other people's religious views does not mean that you must apologize for the hope that you have in Christ or the conviction you have that He alone is Lord. Instead, be consistent in your behavior toward others who believe differently than you, and always show love in your actions towards them.

4. **Walk in their shoes**—try to remember what it was like before you knew Christ. Remember how foolish the Gospel message seemed to you? Your co-workers are in that same place. They may not understand your faith and may find it confusing. Your ability to speak their language with understanding and empathy will go a long way in breaking down barriers that exist between very diverse people.

This is exactly what Jean did when confronted by a co-worker who was angry with her about what she perceived was a major infraction. She accused Jean of talking to a client about religion. Jean was stunned by the accusation because she didn't recall talking with any of their clients about religion and, therefore, asked her co-worker what caused her to believe that she had. Her co-worker responded by saying, "There is a man at the counter who was here yesterday. He wants to talk to the lady who helped him. He can't remember her name but he knows she is a Christian. How would he know if you didn't tell him?"

Jean smiled because she did remember helping a man the previous day, and she went to the counter to greet him again. After she assisted him with a form that he had lost, he left saying, "God bless you." She replied, "God bless you, too."

When she returned to her desk, three of her co-workers were there, all telling her that she needed to be careful because she could be fired for talking religion. She explained that she hadn't said a word to the man about her faith. Instead she told them that the Bible tells us that we will know our fellow Christians by their spirit, actions, their kindness, gentleness, and love. She told them she didn't have to talk to the man about religion, because she simply allowed her light to shine with God's love, and he could see it. However, Jean was puzzled. She asked the co-worker who had initially accused her, "Why did you come to my desk and assume I was the one who helped the man yesterday?" Her co-worker looked at her and then laughed while saying, "Jean, it's just the way you are. I just knew."

Jean ended up having an opportunity to witness to her three co-workers that day and later had lunch with them and shared the gospel over lunch. She would be the first to say that you don't have to beat people over the head with words or put guilt trips on anyone. You only have to live what you believe, and they will know.

Ultimately it is what you do rather than what you say that will have the greatest impact in your workplace. As you appreciate the diversity of your co-workers, you will find that there are many different ways to serve God, and one of them is by learning to embrace the differences inherent in all people. As you do, you will discover that you may have many other things in common with those who believe differently than you do. Ask God to help you leverage those commonalities to develop relationships that may, one day, lead to an opportunity for you to share your faith. People will listen to those whom they trust. Trust is developed over time and comes after strong relationships have been established. Don't let the differences that exist between you and others at work overshadow all the ways that you may complement one another. We are all made uniquely in God's image, each serving a very specific purpose that only we were designed to achieve. Who knows—the differences that you and your co-workers have regarding faith may be just the segue that God uses to reveal Himself like never before.

Diversity is one of the buzzwords in today's workplace. But it is not new to God and to the person of faith; it is just another way to celebrate who He is.

Chapter Five

Seek Help and Wisdom

Faith at Work Tip: Consult with God before consulting with anyone else

Wisdom is the principal thing; therefore get wisdom. And in all your getting, get understanding (Proverbs 4:7).

It doesn't take long to realize, as a person of faith, that you are sharply outnumbered at work. The average work place has few attributes of faith in it, and people who have a desire to demonstrate their faith while at work will be challenged. A good example of this happened recently to Brenda. Brenda thought it would be a great idea to have a Bible study group meet at work before the beginning of the workday. She felt it would be an opportunity for believers to get together, study God's word, and be an encouragement to one another. She also planned to spend a portion of the time praying for their employer, petitioning God to help the business to be successful.

The only request that Brenda made of her company was permission to use a conference room at the office. She was very specific in stating in her request that the conference room would be needed for only the 30 minutes prior to the start of the workday and that the meetings would never conflict with any business-related needs. She went through the appropriate channels and explained the group's purpose, being certain to point out that this would be a purely voluntary gathering and that everyone was welcome to come.

Imagine Brenda's disappointment when her employer soundly refused her request to use a conference room for the purpose of religious activities. Even though the company frequently allowed others to use their facilities for other non-work related activities, her request was viewed with suspicion because of the nature of the proposed group.

Stories like this one illustrate some of the reasons people of faith often feel they are outnumbered and misunderstood, as well as feeling that they are treated differently from others, especially in a business climate that is becoming increasingly non-tolerant of expressions of religious beliefs. But the truth of the matter is that we are not outnumbered. Any time God is involved, the odds change, and we have a distinct advantage that is supernatural. But how do believers learn to have confidence about their being in the majority? A good place to start is to learn to seek God's help and wisdom.

Work was God's idea from the very beginning. God was the first employer. After He made Adam, He gave him a job. Adam's first job was working as a gardener. He was responsible for the upkeep of the Garden of Eden (Genesis 1:15). Later, God gave Adam another work assignment. He was responsible for giving names to all of the other living creatures (Genesis 2:19). These were pretty cushy jobs and didn't require much effort on Adam's part. However, after Adam disobeyed God, he was given his toughest work assignment. He had to farm the land in order to survive. From that day until the present, people have been working to earn a living, and history has shown that working with wisdom and knowledge is critical to performing well under any circumstance.

When we look back at the heroes of our faith, we see that their attributes of wisdom and knowledge were essential to their successes. The same will be true for any task that we undertake. Starting with Daniel, we discover a young man who was given extraordinary wisdom and understanding by God. Remember the story of the King's dream in the second chapter of Daniel? King Nebuchadnezzar had a very disturbing dream, but when he awoke from it, he couldn't remember the details of it or understand what it meant. As a result, he called all of the wise men in his kingdom together and asked them to tell him what he had dreamed and what it meant. It would have been an impossible task for an ordinary person, but it was alleged that the men had mystical powers, yet they could not deliver the results that the king demanded. As a result, the king decided that all of the wise men of the kingdom were to be killed. This news of course reached Daniel, who was not aware of what had happened until he received word that he and his three friends were to be killed, too. Daniel immediately went to see the king to ask him for some time to determine what his dream had been. Immediately after being granted the additional time he needed, Daniel went home and gathered his three friends together, and they asked God to help them.

Of course, you know the rest of the story. God not only told Daniel what the king had dreamed but also told him exactly what the dream meant. As a result, Daniel was able to advise the king on a matter of great importance. This resulted in Daniel's rise to great prominence within the kingdom. Does God still help today's believer in the workplace in such a dramatic fashion? Absolutely! At work, we are challenged every day to solve problems that can impact our employer's ability to be profitable. And even when those problems aren't complicated, we still must know how to perform the basic skills and tasks necessary to do our jobs. Gaining the wisdom and knowledge needed to excel at their work should be the desire of all persons of faith. We should also feel confident that we can request this knowledge and wisdom from God and that He will provide all that we need to perform well. However, this doesn't mean that we are to sit back and wait for the wisdom to pop into our heads. God expects us to learn as much as we can and to seek opportunities for increasing our knowledge.

Several years ago, I had a choice to either remain in a job that I knew like the back of my hand or to work on a project that would require some skills and knowledge that I hadn't fully developed. At first, I almost talked myself out of the assignment because I thought I would be in over my head. But I ultimately wrote down the pros and cons of taking the assignment as a way to help me decide whether or not I should pursue the opportunity. One of the considerations that I gave strong weight to was the ability to learn new skills. I prayed very earnestly for God to direct me in the decision. I knew that if He had provided this opportunity for me to learn something new, He would also provide me with the aptitude to learn the new skills that I needed.

I finally decided to take the challenge, and I accepted the assignment. There were some frightening days ahead—days when I was wondering what I had gotten myself into. At one point, I even thought that I might have made a huge mistake. Because the work was so challenging and the environment was so stressful, I started to doubt that it was God's purpose for me to be on the project in the first place. Some of the members of the project team were especially difficult to work with, and it was becoming a "dog eat dog" type of place. However, one day while I was praying about the situation—asking God for the courage I needed to do my best and for Him to help me to form better working relationships with some of the team members—I received a phone call. It was my brother-in-law calling to encourage me with a very specific scripture. He said, "No weapon formed against you will prosper" (Isaiah 54:17). I had never heard that scripture, and I asked him what it meant. He explained very carefully that all of us have to face difficult circumstances in our lives, which may include someone trying to harm us. He meant not only physical harm but also that people may attempt to damage our reputations, or cause others to believe that we are not competent in our work. They may use words to hurt us in some fashion. Whatever weapon they may choose to use will not have its intended effect because God has promised that it won't. While I was listening to my brother-in-law, I had a "a light bulb turning on in my head" experience. I had been asking God to help me with my project, and He reassured me through these encouraging words that He had everything under control.

As the days of the project passed, my attitude shifted from one of constant worry about how I was doing and what others were thinking about my work, to one of having a new level of confidence. I knew that as long as God was in control of the situation, I could focus on learning and working to the best of my ability. I didn't have to worry about the circumstances (eventually, the circumstances changed, but first, I changed by learning to rely on God). God had taught me an important lesson. Learning something new isn't always easy, but staying within God's purpose is always best. That lesson has helped me in so many difficult work situations. Going through the situation increased my wisdom by learning to trust God and to let Him be in control. I still rely on that lesson and others like it to face new challenges at work.

So what do you do if you lack wisdom and want to make sure that you are working wisely at all times? The solution is simple—ask God for it. "If any of you lacks wisdom, let him ask of God, who gives to all liberally and without reproach, and it will be given to him. But let him ask in faith, with no doubting, for he who doubts is like a wave of the sea driven and tossed by the wind" (James 1:5-6). These are very clear instructions from God's Word. We are to ask God for wisdom, believing that He will give it to us and that He will give us as much and even more than what is needed, without any negative consequences. Obviously, God's desire is for the believer to freely ask for wisdom because He knows how critical it is for us to operate out of wisdom in every area of our lives, and our work is no exception.

Having wisdom is one thing, but have you ever been in a situation at work where you just needed God's immediate help? Maybe the situation involves a difficult work relationship that seems irreparable or a task that you cannot figure out, or maybe it involves a customer who always has some problem that requires untangling. In the midst of trying to do your best, have you ever thought that things had become a mess and you needed God's help. Some friends of mine found themselves in exactly that place.

Bob and Deborah began a roofing business in the late 70s. They had determined they would run their business with honesty and integrity. Despite having had a slow start, they were making a profit a few short years after the business was created. A few years ago, they were faced with a fraudulent lawsuit from someone who had worked for them for only two days. As a result of their attempt to defend themselves, they were in a downward spiral of debt. During the next few years, their debt to their supplier gradually grew from an amount that averaged between $15,000 and $20,000, to one that averaged more than $120,000. As believers, they had operated with integrity toward their supplier. They never tried to hide from their supplier and always assured him of their desire to pay their debt. There were many times after they had looked to God for help that they knew He had given them divine favor with their supplier because their credit was not cut off, which would have shut down their business permanently. Even when the supplier received pressure from headquarters, they always stood with Bob and Deborah and vouched for them, placing their own reputation on the line many times.

For seven years, Bob and Deborah worked on paying off that debt. One day, they received a phone call from their supplier's headquarters, notifying them they still owed $71,000 and asking them if they could make a substantial payment toward the debt. After praying about it and asking for God's help, Bob and Deborah managed to pull together enough money to pay the supplier $20,000. The supplier responded by telling them that if they were willing to do that, the supplier was willing to cancel the remaining $51,000 of the debt! The blessing they received was not only the $51,000 but also the interest that went along with it, making the true value of the blessing nearly $100,000.

When I asked Bob and Deborah what they believed to be the reason God had helped them in such a phenomenal manner, they responded by saying, "When a man's ways please the Lord, He makes even his enemies to be at peace with him" (Proverbs 16:7). Their supplier was not their enemy, but debt was. They had always tried to be obedient to God in all their business dealings. They never cheated or deceived any of their customers or employees. They always looked for ways to bless others and to help them. They volunteered at their church and always supported the ministry of their church. These were all ways that they had lived their life to honor God. As a result, when they called out for help, God responded in a magnificent way.

What I love most about God is that He is the master at dealing with impossible situations or those situations where we simply do not have a clue as to what we should do. Some people may read the story of Bob and Deborah and think that the outcome was just a coincidence. I have heard it said that a coincidence is merely God's decision to remain anonymous. That may be true for those who believe in coincidences. I happen to believe that nothing happens by chance. I think there was a direct correlation to the way Bob and Deborah ran their business and the willingness of their supplier to forgive their debt. That correlation was God. He was the one who gave them favor with their supplier. He was the one was caused the supplier to have a complete change of heart and decide to cancel out their debt. He was the one who answered when they cried out for help, and He was the one who took action.

As believers and people of faith, we can always feel comfortable that our requests for help from God do not go unnoticed. In fact, He expects us to seek His direction, and He wants us to turn to Him with our impossible situations. I am reminded of how different our perspective is from His. Often our thinking of circumstances as being so hard and so difficult usually results from our tendency to look at our situation and not at the size of our God. While walking in the park recently, I overheard a small boy giving instructions to his father while practicing kicks with him on a soccer field. The little boy and a friend were taking turns kicking the ball towards the net in an attempt to make a goal. His dad was the goalie and was standing in front of the soccer net blocking the kicks. The conversation went something like this:

The little boy said, "Dad, you need to be careful cause Denney is our best kicker! He could hurt you, Dad, so you need to watch out!"

The father chuckled and said, "OK, Son, I'll watch out for him."

"I'm not kidding, Dad. Denney is very good. You had better get ready cause he kicks really hard."

At this point, I turned to watch the famous Denney as he ran towards the ball and kicked it solidly past his friend's father directly into the net. It was also at this point that I noticed that the father seemed to have purposely stepped aside just a little to give Denney the opportunity to get the ball in. His little son shook his head sorrowfully and said, "Dad, I tried to warn you. Didn't I tell you that Denney was good?" Anyone watching this scene would have laughed as I did. It was obvious to everyone but the little boy that Denney was no match for the much taller, stronger man. In fact, we could all see that the father was simply allowing Denney to save face in front of his son. He clearly could have blocked that ball with one hand tied behind his back, but simply chose not to.

As I reflected on this incident, I thought about how often my perspective on my problems is just like the little boy's was. We see a big problem, and we try to warn God that this may be the toughest situation He has had to face. How do we warn God? We do so by worrying about problems, by refusing to ask for help, and by trying to solve them ourselves. In essence, we are saying, "God this is too big for you to handle. I need to figure this out on my own." We, like the boy, see situations from our vantage point. I'm sure the little boy had played against his friend many times on the soccer field and had become accustomed to being out-kicked. Having never been an adult, he had no way to see his friend from an adult's perspective, so he did what came natural to him. He warned his father about his friend's capabilities.

Just as it was ridiculous for the little boy to think that his friend was a true match for his father, it is ridiculous for us to think that there is a problem at work that is too big for God. It's all about perspective. We look at a situation from our limited view, our limited perspective, and with no way of knowing all the factors involved. God, on the other hand, sees the entire scope of the matter. He knows how the problem was created in the first place, and as a result, knows exactly what is needed to fix it. As we gain an understanding of this truth, we realize how critical it is for us to stop trying to do that which only God can do and to focus on those things that we have the ability to solve.

In a day and time when true wisdom and knowledge are scarce at best, knowing that we have a God in heaven who cares about our affairs and is willing to help us should make us realize that we have a great champion in our corner. No, we are not outnumbered. Once we recognize God as our source and learn to rely on Him, there is no problem too difficult to solve, and wisdom will be our guide.

PART TWO

Godly Principles for Career Success

I believe everyone who has ever worked wishes there were some sure-fire ways to guarantee success. No matter what type of work we do, we typically want to be paid well and be recognized for a job well done. Most people don't go to work with the idea of doing their jobs badly, and people of faith are no exception. Wouldn't it be wonderful if there were some principles that would guide us in our quest for career success? Of course, many books have been written on the subject, and there are many consultants who have full time jobs advising others about achieving success in their careers. However, most of this guidance deals with the external person and not the internal person. It seems to completely ignore the obvious, which is that we are not just physical or mental beings. We are also spiritual beings, and any form of guidance needs to take this factor into consideration.

In this section, there are seven principles that I believe will lead you to the kind of success that only God can give. Of course, there will be some practical examples which focus on the many aspects of who we are and ways that we can use our energies to progress within our careers. But more importantly, we will discuss what must happen on the inside—to our spirits—to increase our chances of achieving success at work as God would define it.

As we examine the lives of Daniel and his contemporaries, as well as modern day women and men of faith, we will see that God has already created a road map for us to follow. You see, God wants us to have success in our work. He wants us to model excellence in the workplace, recognizing that our greatest testimony to others may be how well we execute the responsibilities that we are given at work. In fact, we are encouraged to not work "as unto men, but as unto the Lord" (Colossians 3:23). With Him as our ultimate employer, we can take direction from the best to be the best.

Chapter Six

Principle 1—Dress for Success

Faith at Work Tip: Never leave home without your armor

Put on the whole armor of God, that you may be able to stand against the wiles of the devil (Ephesians 6:11).

Jennifer is an executive coach who works with many senior level executives in various corporations throughout the United States. She helps her professional clients in the same way that a sports coach would help an athlete—by providing them with the necessary counsel and advice to improve their performance and encourage a different approach for improved personal effectiveness. She shared a story with me about one client, Sue, who was having a difficult time working with another colleague. In their discussions, it became apparent to Jennifer that her client was totally intimidated by a male colleague and often felt useless and demoralized after any interactions with him. He was what is commonly known in professional circles as an "office bully." He never missed the opportunity to ridicule her ideas or to speak louder than her at meetings. He also managed to discount any suggestions that she made in the presence of others.

As a result, Sue often came home after a day at the office feeling worthless and doubting her ability to make a real contribution to her team. Jennifer began coaching Sue on techniques to remind her of all the significant successes that she had had in the past. It was these successes that had qualified her for the very responsible position that she was currently in. She started by suggesting that before going to the office each day, Sue should visualize putting on a cloak. The cloak was to have on it gold medals for past successes, creative ideas that had been implemented, and suggestions she had made that had been acknowledged and approved by her superiors. She told Sue that if at any time the office bully began to cause her to feel undervalued, then she was to visualize her cloak as a protective covering that he could not invade. It would serve as a reminder to her of who she was and why her work was valuable despite what he said.

As Sue began to implement this strategy, she felt herself becoming stronger every day. Every time she had a confrontation with her male colleague, she envisioned her cloak and remembered that she was a valuable member of the team. She would then begin to be more forceful in responding to some of his criticisms, and the confidence that had waned, quickly returned. Sue used a professional visualization technique that could be referred to as "dressing for success." By seeing herself in a cloak of her past successes, it became difficult for her colleague to get through her armor, and as a result, his attacks had minimal effect.

This episode reminded me of a book entitled *Dress for Success* that I read early in my career. The author spoke of the importance of going to work dressed in the attire of the type of job in which you hoped to be, rather than being dressed for the type of job you had. For example, if you were a clerical worker and hoped to one day be in a professional position, he encouraged you to dress as though you were already in the professional job. His premise was that visual impressions are so important that people assign value to you based on the way you are dressed. If they see you in a suit, they will see you as a professional worker. Whereas, if they see you in clothes that are less business-like, they will assume your work role is less important.

When Sue began to dress in her success cloak each day, it changed her countenance. Although there wasn't an actual cloak that others could see, they could see that something was different about her because she had begun to see herself differently. The way she saw herself impacted the way others saw her as well. As a result, she began to experience success again in her work, and the dynamics between her and her colleague also began to change. They started to operate more as peers than as a bully and a victim.

As people of faith, we are also encouraged to dress for success.

There is a spiritual bully who spends all his time attempting to make us feel useless and unimportant. He tries to cut us down and make us doubt the value that we bring to the workplace. Whether it is through people or through circumstances, he prowls around to see if there is even the slightest chink in our armor, and when he finds it, that is where he begins his attack. The sad part of it is that he uses the same tactics over and over again. The same was true in Daniel's time. After he enjoyed a successful career during the reign of King Nebuchadnezzar, it appeared as though Daniel's success had come to a grinding halt following the death of the king.

For many years after the king's death, Daniel worked in obscurity, basically an unknown to the new leader of Babylon. During these years, it would have been easy for Daniel to believe that his work was no longer important and that he was not a valuable member of the team. Instead, he continued on faithfully doing his job and being committed to dressing for success every day. He didn't allow his circumstances at work to change his commitment to serving God. He continued to pray and serve God by being faithful to the work he had been given to do. Just as it was in Daniel's day, so it is today. In order to be prepared for whatever circumstances come our way at work, we, too, must learn to dress for success. Like Sue and Daniel, we must visualize putting on a cloak—our armor—every day before entering our places of work. But what does this armor look like?

There is a great passage in Ephesians that describes the clothing, or armor, as it is referred to in the Bible, that we are to put on every day. In order to dress for success at work, we must have five items of clothing, which are essential to our workplace success.

1. Truth

This is possibly the most important item of clothing that you can have on at work. Truth sets us apart from so many others that we will come into contact with at work. Knowing the truth about God, knowing the truth about ourselves, and knowing the truth about others will give us an advantage at work because we will be able to know what is really going on through our spiritual senses, and not simply based on what we see. If we know the truth about God, then we know that He is greater than our circumstances, He has a good plan for our lives, He loves us, and He cares about what happens to us. If we know the truth about ourselves, then we know that we were created to worship God; our lives do not belong to us, but to Him; and when we give ourselves to Christ, we can do anything that we are destined to do because He lives in us. Finally, when we know the truth about others, we realize that they, too, were created by God, and whether they recognize it or not, they were created to worship Him and to serve Him. We know that God expects us to treat others the way we would want to be treated since they ultimately belong to Him.

There is power in walking in the truth because it causes us to act differently and respond differently. When you really believe that you can do all things because Christ lives in you, what impact does that have on your work each day? If you believe that God is bigger than your circumstances at work, whether that may involve a lay-off, a promotion not received, or working with a difficult boss, how will believing this truth change your response to those circumstances? It becomes easier to see that putting on the truth each day will determine the level of success at which you will handle your work.

2. Righteousness

This item of clothing speaks more about our standing with God. We are righteous because of what Christ did for us on the cross. Because we are righteous, we don't have to live with past regrets or be burdened by the guilt of past sins. Of course, we will still experience some failure, but we know that God's mercy is new every day. As we begin to know that we are in right standing with God through Christ, we can handle our failures with the security of knowing that everything will work together for our good.

3. Peace

Experiencing peace at work can often be a challenge. You may even be thinking that it's your job that keeps you from having peace. However, this is another essential component of our dress uniform for success at work. We are told in the Scriptures that we are not to be anxious about anything, but that instead we are to pray about everything and make our requests known to God. We are assured that when we do this, the peace of God, which is beyond anything we can understand, will be ours. How much more effective could we be at work if each day we started out with a dose of God's peace? Imagine the deadlines we could complete without all the drama. Imagine the calmness we could experience when our daily agenda was changed at the last minute to new priorities outside of our control. Or what about the irate customers that we could calm down if peace reigned in our own hearts? Having God's peace, not just any peace, makes a world of difference in how we execute our daily responsibilities. Because it is supernatural, we will find ourselves capable of accomplishing so much more than our normal capabilities, despite having difficult situations or difficult people at work.

4. Faith

Did you know that it is impossible to please God without faith? In fact, with faith, we can speak to those mountains in our lives, those circumstances that are outside of our control, and tell them to get lost; and because of faith, they have to go. But this kind of faith is not just believing in anything; instead, it is the faith that believes God is who He says He is and that God can do anything He says He can do. With this in mind, we know that we cannot leave home and go to work without first putting on our shield of faith. It is this shield that helps us deal with those impossible situations at work. When we have faith that God is in control, despite how things may look, we know that we will ultimately be victorious and will experience the success that only God can give. It is faith that sustains us during the difficult times because faith is the substance of things hoped for, and it is the evidence of things not yet seen. Think about those things that you may be dealing with at work today. What is in your circumstances that you need to believe God for? Do you need to believe that God is going to touch your boss's heart and cause him or her to change their mind about a decision that is important to you? Do you need to believe that God is working in a situation even though there doesn't appear to be any evidence that He cares about it as much as you do? Maybe you need to believe that God will change you into a person who can really make a difference in her workplace? Whatever your need is, it all starts with faith. When we have a faith that believes God is who He says He is and that He can do what He says He can do, we will begin to experience success in our lives and our work because we know that we are pleasing God.

5. Salvation

A really good suit of armor always has a protective piece to cover the head. That, in effect, is what salvation through Christ does for the true believer. It provides a covering that sustains the believer day in and day out. For it is salvation through Christ that gives the believer the power of God's spirit and, therefore, makes the believer able to accomplish feats at work that normally would not result from human effort alone. Who could really love (as God commands) a colleague who is hard to get along with, if they simply tried to love through their own effort? Most of us would agree that it would be an impossible assignment at best, especially if we began to think about those colleagues that really drive us crazy. However, through salvation in Christ, day by day we take on His character as we let His nature replace our human nature. God gives His power along with salvation, causing us to successfully demonstrate His love in the workplace. It is also His saving power that convicts us when we have fallen back into old bad habits that need to be corrected. It is salvation in Christ lived out in the life of a believer that makes the Gospel real at work and reassures us that no matter what we face, our destiny in Christ has already been determined and our futures are certain.

6. Word of God

Each of the items of clothing we have discussed so far is important and essential. This piece of armor, however, is critical. Knowing what God says in His Word, the Bible, and applying that knowledge daily at work is the key to our success. How can we know the truth if we don't know God's Word? How can we have peace if we don't know how to obtain it? How can we be righteous unless we read where God tells us that we are righteous through Christ? How can we obtain faith without knowing God's Word? And how would we know of God's plan for our salvation and life eternal with Him if we didn't first read His marvelous promises in His Word? The fact is that every piece of spiritual clothing that we put on is stitched together by the Word of God. It is the Word that creates the fabric of our armor, and it is the Word that causes us to live and work successfully according to God's plan for our lives.

My friend Ann shared a story with me that revealed that dressing for success really works. Ann has a longtime friend, Annabelle, who is also a believer. Annabelle had worked for her organization for more than five years and her boss had been with the company for slightly under three years. In the beginning of their work relationship, Annabelle and her boss seemed to get along well. But one day, for no apparent reason, something changed in their relationship. Although Annabelle tried several times to pinpoint just what had caused the change, she was never able to do so. She went from being her boss's confidant, to being considered one of her worst employees. Everything Annabelle did seemed to upset her boss in some way. She questioned all of Annabelle's decisions and even accused Annabelle of falsifying her mileage records. Annabelle said there was only one thing that sustained her during this time: her faith.

The stress at work had become so difficult for her that Annabelle sought the counsel of her employer's EAP. During her visits with the EAP counselor, she shared her beliefs and some passages of scripture that gave her strength. One of those passages was Deuteronomy 31:8 which says, "And the Lord, He is the One who goes before you. He will be with you; He will not leave you nor forsake you; do not fear nor be dismayed." Annabelle shared that it was this passage that helped her decide to remain at her job. Having been counseled to consider changing jobs, Annabelle stated emphatically, "I'm staying. God still has something for me to do here, and when that is completed, then He will lead me to my next assignment." She knew that God was in her corner, and she believed that He would do exactly what He said he would.

As a result, Annabelle has continued to work at that same job with her same boss, and amazingly, the environment, as well as their relationship, has improved. She is a living example of dressing for success. She understood the truth about God, herself, and others. She accepted that she was righteous before God due to her relationship with Christ. She had faith that God is who He says He is and can do what He says he can do. She acknowledged Christ as Lord of her life by deciding not to just take the easier path of leaving her job but to instead seek His guidance about that important decision. And most importantly, she knew God's Word and confessed it in her circumstances. It was the power in His Word that gave her the courage to stick with it even when the situation looked desperate.

We too have the opportunity to choose to dress for success each day before we enter the workplace. It is a choice that must be made daily. We can go to work with the attitude that nothing will ever change and our situations are hopeless or we can go to work believing that God is in control of every aspect of our lives and has our situations in hand. We can believe that we will never be able to make valuable contributions at our workplace or we can choose to believe that all things are possible with God. It is our choice. Annabelle learned the value of choosing to dress for success daily and so did Daniel. And so can you.

Chapter Seven

Principle 2—
Recognize the Source of Your Talents

Faith at Work Tip: Use your talents to bless others

As each one has received a gift, minister it to one another, as good stewards of the manifold grace of God (1 Peter 4:10).

During the late nineteenth century, yellow fever was one of the most deadly diseases of the time. During the Spanish American War thousands of soldiers died in Cuba as a result of the spread of the disease. Walter Reed was a young army surgeon who was sent to Cuba to determine what was causing the outbreak of yellow fever. Leading a team of doctors, he proved through experiments that yellow fever is transmitted by mosquitoes and not by direct contact with those who are infected (which was the common belief at the time). Within three months, yellow fever had been virtually eradicated due to Dr. Reed's work. Despite receiving honors and world acclaim as a result of his discovery, Dr. Reed continued to credit God with giving him the wisdom that ultimately inspired his work.

Each of us is born with certain talents and abilities. Some of those talents require nurturing and development, but they are already there simply waiting to be discovered. From the time we were created, these amazing gifts were placed within us, and after we were born they begin to be refined as we discovered them and put them to use. When we become aware of this simple truth, we begin to seek out opportunities that help us to grow and develop. It is God who places those talents and abilities in us at the time we are created. Success at work requires that we acknowledge our gifts and begin to seek ways that we can purposefully use them.

When Daniel first arrived at work, he immediately began to recognize that he had certain gifts, which he might not have been aware of prior to starting his first job. After all, he was a quick learner, which enabled him to learn on the fly. He possessed great wisdom, which allowed him to be a good decision-maker; and he had good instincts, which caused him to know how to best serve his boss and his constituents. In addition, he had an intellect that was far superior to those of his colleagues, and he had the ability to interpret how future events would impact his boss's franchise.

With all these talents, it would have been easy for Daniel to become puffed up and full of pride, but time and again, he demonstrated that he recognized where his gifts came from and developed into one of the strongest servant leaders of his time. Daniel consistently practiced three habits that served to remind him of the source of his talents and abilities. First, he continually made God the focus of his life. Second, he always gave credit to God for his successes. Finally, he developed a strong prayer life and, therefore, stayed in constant communication with God.

When we begin thinking about our own talents and abilities, we, too, can acknowledge the giver of these gifts by developing the same habits that Daniel did.

Make God the Focus of Your Life

This requires determination on our part. There should not be a day that we don't thank God for the talent He has given us to do our jobs. In fact, it's a great idea to wake up each morning thanking God for the ability to go to work and to be able to do whatever task is set before us. This will serve as a reminder that without Him, we would have nothing at all.

We can also seek ways to use our talents to serve others. By doing this, we set in motion a universal spiritual law that says we will reap what we sow. As we sow our talents into the lives of others, we will continue to reap more talent so that we can continue to serve. This is a natural outcome of a life totally focused on serving God.

Most importantly we must avoid compromising our talents and

abilities. Our gifts weren't given to us to be abused. Say for instance that you have a gift that allows you to be very smart about money matters, it should never be used to purposefully deceive those who may not be as smart in those same matters but have placed their trust in you. By not compromising, we continue to acknowledge that our talent does not belong to us to do with as we please but is better described as on loan to do the work that we have been assigned to do.

Always Give Credit Where Credit is Due

It's no secret that some of the amazing things that happened in Daniel's career practically shouted out to others: God at work here! However, to ensure that there was no mistaking who was responsible for his phenomenal performance, Daniel always let those around him know where the credit truly belonged. We have the opportunity to do the same. Sometimes this will involve acknowledging God's help as Daniel did, and other times it will involve us acknowledging the contributions of others. Have you ever noticed that when an audience gives the conductor of an orchestra a standing ovation, the conductor immediately stands, bows, and then turns to acknowledge the concertmaster and the other musicians—always encouraging them to stand as well? The conductor is acknowledging that he is only part of a team of people that caused the beautiful music of the orchestra. If our talent has been enhanced by the actions of others, it is important that we say so and let others share in our success. Humility is revealed by acknowledging the greatness of others, and by doing so, we show the heart of God through our actions.

Develop a Lifestyle of Prayer

One of the most important habits that Daniel developed was a very active prayer life. This is a habit well worth emulating. When we pray, we open up a channel that is best described as an ongoing dialogue. During those times of prayer, we can recognize God for who He is, and it will serve as a reminder to us of who we are—people totally dependent on Him. It is during prayer time that we gain strength and wisdom to know how to use the talents and abilities that we have been given and to learn to be disciplined in doing the work that we must do each day. When we pray, we acknowledge that God is the giver of all things, and we begin to learn that He wants to continue to give good things to us, so that we will be well qualified to do the work that He has for us to do.

One of my first paying jobs, while still a teenager, was working as a part-time hostess at a local pancake house. Despite being very young, I was able to obtain the position through a family friend. The restaurant manager had some reservations about hiring me because I had no experience working in a restaurant. He decided to give me a chance because of our friend's recommendation.

I loved that job! I loved everything about it. I loved talking to the customers, setting up the stations, filling up the salt-and-pepper shakers, and I didn't mind bussing tables when necessary. But I especially loved getting tips. It was gratifying to know that simply by being nice to people and serving them food, I would be rewarded. Initially, since I didn't have a station assigned to me, I would receive tips only when helping out the waitresses. I had the morning shift and would have regular customers that came in every morning for breakfast. Because I saw some of these customers practically every day, we eventually became friends. No matter which station I happened to be working, my regulars would ask to be seated at that station. They were great tippers, and of course, I was delighted!

One day, while I was serving a customer, the restaurant manager called me over and said, "You know, I didn't think you were going to work out when I first hired you since you had no experience, but you seem to have a natural talent for this job. Keep up the good work." That was literally my first performance review, and I was promoted to the position of waitress. Oh happy day—tips galore! I absolutely excelled as a waitress, and before I knew it, I had been assigned one of the largest stations, which allowed me to have even more customers, and of course, perfect my talent.

The memories of those days are still with me, and I always think of them with great fondness. For it was during that time that I began to discover where talent and ability really come from. Think about it—I had never worked in a restaurant. No one had given me the slightest hint about being a hostess or waiting on tables. Obviously, there were some things I had to learn on the job, for instance, using the cash register, learning the menu items, and so on. But ultimately, my success involved some skills that I was born with, and one of them happened to be serving others. Having this ability helped me to be successful as a waitress, and it continues to be a very important skill to me today.

Acknowledging that our talents and abilities come from God does something else for us as well. It develops in us a spirit of humility. Since we know that God will often use our work situations to continue to build our character, we can expect to see events occur that will challenge us to remain humble no matter how talented we may be. In fact, we are admonished to be "clothed in humility" (1 Peter 5:5), and the best way to sustain that is to constantly remind ourselves that our talents don't belong to us; they are gifts from God.

Finally, acknowledging that our talents and abilities come from God helps us to be successful in our work. The success that comes to a person of faith who is completely relying on God in all their work will be success that provides the peace and dignity that always results from a job well done. We know that there will always be someone who can work harder and longer than we can. There will be those who work as though they are in a race to obtain a prize—the ones who set the curve for everyone else. Our goal should be more substantial than that. Our goal should be to take the talent we have been given and use it in a way that accomplishes the purpose for which God gave it to us.

I am reminded of a story that I once heard about the great football coach Bear Bryant. While Alabama was playing Auburn, the first string quarterback became injured, and Coach Bryant had to bring in the second string quarterback. The game was very close, and there was not much time left on the clock. Even though Alabama had a slight lead and possession of the ball, the coach didn't want to risk losing the game due to a mistake at the very end. So he told the second-string quarterback, "No matter what you do during these last seconds of the game, do not pass that ball." As the teams begin to play, the quarterback remembered what his coach had told him, and he didn't pass the ball. However, there came a point in the game where he saw that his wide receiver was open and ready to receive a pass, so he passed the ball. What he didn't see was that one of Auburn's fastest players was also waiting to see if the football would be passed, and as soon as the quarterback released the ball, the Auburn player intercepted it and started running towards the goal line. The Alabama second-string quarterback was not very fast and was certainly no match for the Auburn player, but somehow, he was not only able to catch up with him but he was also able to tackle him and retrieve the ball. Alabama won the game! Later, when Coach Bryant was approached by the media, he was asked why it was that his quarterback was able to run so fast that day although he was known to be one of his slowest players. The coach smiled slowly and said, "Well, you see, that other player was just running to reach the goal line; my player was running for his life."

That's true of the believer too. While those who are running for the goal line may surround us, we are in fact running for our lives. God has given us certain gifts that help us to run the race that has eternal value. Not only should we seek to develop those gifts, but also we should always seek to use them in the way, and with the purpose for which they were designed.

By acknowledging God's role in providing him with his extraordinary gifts, Daniel continued to succeed, while others fell by the wayside. As we acknowledge God's role in providing our talents and abilities, we will, like Daniel, continue to experience success.

Chapter Eight

Principle 3—Achieve Excellence

Faith at Work Tip: Demonstrate the excellence of God through the excellence of your work

Therefore, my beloved brethren, be steadfast, immovable, always abounding in the work of the Lord, knowing that your labor is not in vain in the Lord (1 Corinthians 15:58).

There are very few companies that I like more than Southwest Airlines. Since I travel a lot, I have learned to appreciate those airlines that take good care of their customers. Southwest Airlines does that very effectively. But Southwest Airlines is not just a company, it is a company made up of people who are committed to excellence. I came face to face with this commitment one Thanksgiving holiday. My family and I were traveling to visit relatives. We were very excited about spending the holidays with our loved ones and were anxious to get to our destination. We arrived at the airport with plenty of time to spare. Upon arriving at the check-in counter, we were dismayed to learn the plane had been overbooked and there were at least 15 passengers who wouldn't have seats on the aircraft. To add insult to injury, we were among the fifteen.

As you can imagine, chaos broke out at as the 15 seatless people began to protest the unfairness of selling more seats than the plane had during a holiday weekend. I must admit that I was right in the thick of things, expressing my disappointment along with the others and trying to figure out what we were going to do to get to our destination. In spite of having to face a little mob, the Southwest Airlines representative remained sympathetic, compassionate, and kind. She worked very hard to get everyone rerouted on the next available flights. But what really stunned me was that she said passengers would not only be reimbursed for the cost of the tickets due to the inconvenience but also would be given free vouchers for travel to anywhere the airlines flew. It was amazing to watch her turn this very angry crowd into people who acted as if they had just won the lottery.

Everything about this woman exhibited qualities of excellence. She didn't try to argue with the customers but made it clear from the beginning that she was on our side. She listened patiently and used a very reassuring tone even when others weren't being as kind as she. It was as though she saw herself as an emissary for her company and wanted to be sure that this one bad experience wouldn't be the last impression that we had of her firm. As a result, I left the experience convinced that the airline is one of the best-run companies I've encountered. And I came to that conclusion because of the actions of one individual.

Unfortunately, I have also had experiences at the other end of the spectrum. One particular rental-car agency comes to mind. I was traveling again with my family. We had a car reservation with this company and arrived at the rental counter to pick it up. The representative on duty was on the phone, and based on the snatches of conversation I overheard, it was a personal call. Despite our appearance at the counter, she continued to conduct her phone conversation and rolled her eyes when I politely said, "Excuse me, but could you help us please?" Reluctantly hanging up, she informed us after searching the computer for our names that she didn't show a reservation for us. Always prepared, I pulled out our confirmation number and gave it to her. She rolled her eyes again as she entered the confirmation number into the computer. Finally, she located our reservation but declared, with what appeared to be very little concern, that there were no cars available. "No cars!" I said with some confusion. "How can that be?" "Simple," she replied, "There are NO CARS!" She enunciated the words slowly and loudly as though speaking to a small child. As the conversation continued, it became apparent that she was not interested in finding a solution to our problem or in helping us to locate a car through another rental-car company. Her I-could-not-care-less attitude was very apparent. When I finally left the counter, I knew that I would never willingly rent from that company again.

Everything about the woman demonstrated a lack of excellence. She showed no concern for her customers, she was impatient and rude, and she acted as though she was doing the customers a favor to serve them. She showed no compassion despite the inconvenience her company had created for me by confirming car availability when no cars were available. I left that experience believing that the company was the worst-run company I had ever encountered. And I came to that conclusion because of the actions of one individual.

One of the most important ways to demonstrate our faith in the workplace is to demonstrate God's excellence in all that we do. If you think about it, what better way is there to show honor and reference to a holy God than by faithfully executing our job responsibilities and putting into action the scripture that says, "Work as unto the Lord and not as unto man" (need reference). If we really were to view God as the boss and were to believe that he watches all that we do, then in what ways would we do our jobs differently?

Actually, we have been called to excellence (2 Peter 1:3) by God who desires that we become just like Him. However, it is a journey, not to be confused with attempting to be perfect. Excellence can be demonstrated not only in our actions but also in our hearts' desires to perform a work that is pleasing to God. With this attitude, we will find that it is through our work that we can share and experience the glory of God (John 3:21).

In order to be excellent in all that we do, we have to seek God first each day for the wisdom and knowledge to do our jobs well. That is what Daniel and his friends learned to do early on. Daniel and the other Hebrew boys purposed in their hearts that they were going to always seek God first—before any other thing. There were some specific outcomes in their lives as a result of them taking this approach. It says in the Scriptures that God gave Daniel and his friends knowledge and skill in all learning and wisdom. It also says that there were no other workers as good as Daniel, Shadrach, Meshach, and Abednego. In fact, they performed ten times better than their colleagues did.

Why did God cause them to be so effective? It was simply because they put God ahead of everything else. They wanted to be a part of the work God was doing in their workplace. They didn't see it as only their work. They saw it as God's work, and they were simply participating in the work that He had for them to do. I saw this approach to excellence beautifully demonstrated by a woman I met at a speaking engagement in California. She told me that God had used her teaching career as an opportunity to reveal His love in a very challenging school.

After working for 19 years as a middle school teacher, she felt that her interests were changing and decided to move in a new direction by working as a counselor at an alternative high school. The environment was completely different than the one she was accustomed to. Some of the teens had been in and out of jail, others had had problems at traditional high schools, many were addicted to drugs and alcohol, and many of the girls were teenage mothers. They came to school, but often did so reluctantly or by court order, and very often came having issues.

Every day on her way to work, she would pray for God to use her in such a way that she would reach those kids. Being in a public school, she had to be very careful not to preach or evangelize, yet she knew that what was missing most from those children's lives was the knowledge that God cared about them and had a good plan for them. Each day, she went to work determined to live a Christ-centered life before them, with the hope that it would register with them that they were headed down a dangerous path. She counseled many of the students regarding developing skills that would help them to have a better life. She even sought out another person of faith, a teacher on staff, who agreed to pray with her daily for the students, trusting that someday the young people would turn their lives over to God.

Many years passed and many of the students had either given up on their education and dropped out of school or were expelled, and yet, she continued to faithfully work as a counselor and pray daily for the students. One day, a student, whom she had found particularly difficult, stopped by the school to obtain a copy of her high school transcript. While there, she decided to stop by to visit with her former school counselor. The girl reminded her of the many times she had been called into the counselor's office to be reprimanded for her behavior. She said, "I hated you at the time because you tried to set me straight, but now I understand what you were trying to do." The young woman then told her that she was attending church and had accepted Christ through a university campus ministry. She also invited the counselor to a party that was to be attended by some other former students.

On the day of the party, the counselor drove to the party with the teacher who had been her partner in praying for the students. They couldn't help but wonder who would be there. When they arrived at the house where the party was to be given, they heard laughter as they rang the doorbell, then the door opened as the word "Surprise!" rang out. In the room were many of her worst students, all cleaned up, looking sharp with smiles on their faces. Later, they all shared their personal stories about how they had found God. The party was to thank the counselor and the teacher for caring enough to pray for them and for living a life as silent witnesses to God's love, grace, and mercy.

This story demonstrates that it is our lives that people watch closely. They want to know if we are authentic and if the God we serve is real. This can be revealed to them as we work with excellence and as we share God's love in everything we do, rather than merely in everything we say. Can you remember who was the first person to tell you about God? What impressed you most? Was it their words, or the actions that followed? I can certainly remember all the people whom God has brought along my path and who made an impact on my life. What I remember most about them is the example they lived before me, much more so than the words that they spoke. All of them demonstrated excellence in their work and in the faith they had in God. They gave me an example to follow and added flesh to the God that they served, thus making Him more real to me.

Work As Unto the Lord

Recently, I was amazed to find that people of faith have gotten a bad reputation in some companies because they haven't always worked as unto the Lord. As I talked with different managers and company owners who also happened to be Christians, they described how some of their most difficult employees have been people who professed to be Christians. They shared stories of workers behaving as though they could do less than their best simply because they had the same faith as their bosses. They seemed to have an attitude that said: our goal is heaven so this earthly stuff really isn't that important. While it is true that our goal is heaven, we still have a job to do while on earth. Some of these stories might have been anecdotal, however, they still left me saddened that the actions of a few bad apples might have caused a bad impression of the whole barrel.

So what does it mean to work with excellence as unto the Lord? Does it mean that we have to be perfect? Does it mean that our work will always be better than everyone else's work? Are we absolutely never to be late to work or to have an occasion of calling in sick when we are not feeling well? Of course not. The true meaning of working with excellence is doing our very best and working to the best of our ability. It is an action of the heart as much as it is of the head. In other words, when your heart is set on pleasing God, your actions will follow. Even when your efforts do not win the approval of man, as long as you can look in the mirror and confidently say, "I tried my best before God," then you have demonstrated working with excellence because you would have worked with an excellent heart. A heart set on doing the best possible job and having the intent of accomplishing what has been asked is always one that pleases God. Remember that man looks on the outward appearance, but God always looks at your heart. If your heart is set on excellence, then your actions will follow.

Be Prone to Act

It has been said that a good servant is one who meets the needs of those she serves. However, a great servant is one who anticipates the needs of those she serves and meets them abundantly. As people of faith that want to work with excellence, we must learn to anticipate the needs of others. How many times do we hear someone in the workplace declare, "That's not my job"? Instead of looking for those things that are not in our job description, let us be people who are interested in the small print that says, "and other duties as assigned" and actively look to serve our employers in that way as well. Be prone to action rather than to waiting for someone to tell you what to do and when to do it. Try to think of ways that you can do more than you have been asked to do. If you notice that the copier is out of paper, don't leave it for the next person to add paper. You do it. And while you're at it, check to see if it needs more toner too. If you receive a call from a co-worker's customer, don't just tell them they need to call back and speak to your co-worker. First, determine if there is something that you can do to help in your co-worker's absence, and if there is—do it. It's the little things that demonstrate we are prone to act and have hearts of excellence.

Work Joyfully

There will be days when it is difficult for you to work with joy. But when you find yourself with absolutely nothing to be joyful about, try repeating this:

- Thank God I have a job when so many people do not.
- Thank God I am earning an income when so many people have none.
- Thank God I am physically able to work when so many people are not able to.
- Thank God I have been put in this workplace for this time due to His sovereignty, and He has a plan for my life.
- Thank God I have his favor and blessings in my life and he alone brings me great joy.

When you are able to remind yourself of these things, it is amazing that joy seeps back into your spirit and you begin to recognize that, despite your circumstances, you can learn to work and be content.

Develop Your Personal Slogan

Several years ago, the Ford Motor Company had a catchy slogan they begin using in all their advertisements: Quality Is Job One. This expressed the vision they had for their company, and it was intended to let their employees and customers know that the greatest priority of the company was to produce quality products for their customers. When the company was recently plagued by some highly publicized problems, including the roll-over incidents with the Bridgestone tires, many began to wonder if the slogan being used accurately described the company's true priority.

We should also develop our own personal slogan. It should reflect our vision for our work and our commitment to excellence. It is most important that if we were to advertise it to others, they would be able to recognize by the way our work is carried out that our personal slogan is indeed our priority. What would your slogan say? Would you be able to say what the Apostle Paul said, "I can do all things through Christ who strengthens me"? Or would it be like what Daniel said, "I am resolved not to do anything that displeases God"? Maybe it would be something that you developed entirely on your own, but whatever it is, make sure that it is an accurate reflection of who you are as a person of faith and what you want others to be able to see in you and your work.

When No One Else Is Looking

During the nineteenth century, a sculptor named Frederic Bartholdi worked diligently on a beautiful statue that was to stand 151 feet tall and be a gift from his nation to another country. He and his fellow workmen worked diligently on the statue, using all of their artistic skills to mold each detail of the statue, from its amazing pedestal to its' majestic head. The statue was eventually completed, and now it stands proudly in New York harbor. At the time the Statue of Liberty was built, Mr. Bartholdi did not know that there would be a time when airplanes and helicopters would fly over the head of the statue because air transportation did not exist. As far as he knew, no one would ever see the top of the head of the statue and all of its intricate details. In fact, had he wanted to, he could have left that part undone and no one would have known. And yet, he took pride in doing his job well. When the statue was given a facelift in 1985, the artists responsible for its restoration were totally amazed by the beauty of the design and the painstaking effort that went into each aspect of the crown and the hair on the statue's head. And of course, in the twenty-first century, planes fly overhead daily, and hundreds of passengers are able to share this majestic view. The sculptor did not work to please people. He had a heart for excellence, and at the end of the day, he wanted to be able to look at his work and say, "I did my best."

That is what people of faith have a responsibility to do. In every task we complete, we, too, must set about making it our goal to accomplish it with a heart for excellence. Whether or not anyone ever knows what we have done or takes the time to acknowledge our efforts, we know that our heavenly Father knows all and sees all. It is for His glory that we work, and it is He who sets the standard. Even if no one else is watching, we know He is watching and that He cares about us just as He cared about Daniel. As we go about our work today and everyday, let us remember to work as though God is our employer, let us be prone to act, serving others with joy, knowing that nothing escapes His notice.

Chapter Nine

Principle 4—Never Stop Learning

Faith at Work Tip: Be open to learning new things

But you must continue in the things which you have learned and been assured of, knowing from whom you have learned them...that the man of God may be complete, thoroughly equipped for every good work (2 Timothy 3:14, 17)

While achieving excellence in our work should be the goal of every believer, another one that can make a difference in our success or failure is our willingness to learn. Every day is an opportunity to learn something that we didn't know before. That doesn't mean that we will learn something new every day, but it does means there is always an opportunity to learn if we are looking for it. Don't make the mistake that one of my colleagues made long ago by equating years of experience with amounts of what has been learned.

Deborah had been employed in the marketing department of her company for over a decade. Initially, her ascent had been fast, and she achieved the level of manager within three years. However, once she became the manager, she settled in with no thought given to how she would improve her department or her professional skills. This worked well for a time. She was very good at maintaining the status quo.

However, her company was eventually bought by another firm. She was given high marks by her supervisor and was successful in being placed within the new firm. But very soon afterwards, she started experiencing some difficulty performing her job. She tried using the same methods she had always used to run her department, but her new manager didn't seem at all impressed. Her boss wanted new, innovative, and creative ideas. The ideas Deborah presented were considered to be old school and outdated.

The harder Deborah tried, the more frustrated she became as more of her ideas were shot down, and she began to feel as though her job was in jeopardy. Eventually, it was, and Deborah was demoted to a non-management role. Deborah described the experience to me.

> At first I was deeply humiliated and felt angry because I believed I had been treated unfairly. But as I begin to pray about it and to ask God to help me understand why this had happened, I began to learn that some of the fault actually rested with me. The new manager, who was hired to replace me, really did have a better way of running the department, and her ideas were fresh and new. Although I did so begrudgingly, I finally admitted to myself that I had become complacent. I had stopped learning or growing professionally, and it had taken a toll on the department and had ultimately cost me my job. Although this was a hard lesson to learn, and it was a very painful experience, I am a better person for having gone through it. As a result, I am committed to never letting it happen again.

Admittedly, it would be a difficult lesson for anyone to learn in the fashion that Deborah learned it, but it illustrates the importance of principle four: never stop learning! Every new assignment can be an opportunity to learn something new. And even when it isn't, you can always try new ways of doing routine things to advance your learning. Quite often, many people don't continue to learn because they are afraid of failure. They often think that if they were to try something new it might not work out. Instead, they should think that it might work out. When they begin to think about it from a positive perspective, they realize the possibility of gaining advantages more than outweighs the possibility of failure. While the advantages might be obvious, a few are especially important to consider.

1. **Skills enhancement**—by continuing to learn, you enhance the skills that you already have in addition to learning new ones

I once had an opportunity to be a part of a major project in my firm. The project would require a two-year commitment on my part, and there was no guarantee that I would have a job to come back to once the it was finished. Initially, I was fearful of leaving a sure thing to join a project that might result in no job at all when it was over. However, as I considered the opportunity, I evaluated all the new things I would learn by joining the project. Not only would I be required to use many of the skills I already possessed, but there was also an opportunity to learn an aspect of my profession that I had always wanted to learn all about. After giving it careful consideration and praying about it, I decided to jump on board. One of the deciding factors for me was the opportunity to learn something totally new and different. I can honestly say I have never regretted that decision.

2. **Increased competitive advantage**—if we are really honest with ourselves, we know that the labor market can be very competitive

One of the ways that we can distinguish ourselves is by having more than one tool in our tool kits. In other words, the more things that you know how to do, the more that you have to offer your current employer as well as your potential employers. By continuing to learn, you enhance your skills and become more valuable to your employer, as well as becoming more competitive in the labor market. As you learn new things, you begin to be able to do a number of things well and can ultimately increase your chances of success.

3. **Awareness of new trends**—things are changing constantly in the marketplace, and by being alert to learning new things, we can keep a handle on the trends that are surfacing and prepare ourselves to do new things that might not have existed yesterday

Assuredly, we don't just want to learn new things, we want to learn *the right* new things. Not only will this be helpful to you and how you may do your job today, but it can also be helpful in assisting you to navigate into new arenas that may be surfacing around you.

Just imagine if you had lived during the early twentieth century. As 1899 rolled into 1900, things were beginning to change. If you had had a job as a blacksmith, you could have learned all kinds of new things about being a good blacksmith, but you would have completely missed the mark in terms of what was going on in the marketplace. It was during this time that industrialists such as Henry Ford and James Couzens were beginning to shake things up a bit by mass-producing a new invention called the horseless carriage. At the time, many black-smiths might have thought this was an idea that would never take on any real significance. They might have mistakenly continued to stock up more iron to produce shoes for horses and believed that since they were the best, their customers would never leave them. They would have been wrong.

On the other hand, a blacksmith who was keeping an eye on the trends might have observed the new phenomenon and might have thought that before long everyone might be able to afford one of the new vehicles and then his services would be obsolete. By thinking that way, he would have been able to prepare for the future and have learned an entirely different trade.

4. **Purpose preparation**—this is perhaps the greatest advantage to continuing to learn: gaining experience that prepares you for God's purpose for your life

How many of us can look back on our lives and see that God has woven together our different experiences to prepare us for a work that He has for us today? I know I can, and many others have shared that same experience. One of my favorite examples is the way God used my high school training to prepare me for the work I do today. I went to a high school that specializes in preparing young people for a career in the performing arts. At that time, I had every intention of becoming a great actress. I studied the dramatic arts with great passion and deter-mination. I overcame stage fright and learned to project my voice to the back of a theatre. I learned proper diction and how to use the tone of my voice to set the mood for what was happening around me. I took dance lessons to help me become more graceful on stage and fencing to help my posture and to develop my sense of stage presence. Besides, I just knew that I would need to know how to fence if I were to do any Shakespearean plays because there was always some use for a sword in his plays. After I finished high school, I lost some of my passion for acting and decided to pursue a different course of study in college. I remember wondering why God had allowed me to spend so much time studying drama, since it was apparent that I was never going to use it.

Many years have passed since my high school days, and I smile when I think of how God took everything I learned from those days and began to weave those experiences into my current work. I can't begin to tell you how many times I have had to stand before large groups of people to give a lecture, teach a workshop, or make a presentation that has required all the skills that I acquired so many years ago. I attribute my ease in speaking in front of people to having learned how to overcome stage fright while performing in school. I know that my ability to be heard without a microphone comes from being taught to project my voice from my diaphragm instead of from my throat. You're probably wondering about the fencing. How was God able to weave that in? Well, I'm still waiting to see what He does with that; in the meantime, don't be surprised if some day you see me welding my sword.

The key to all of this is simple. You must be willing to take responsibility for your professional growth. If you want to continue to learn and grow in your work, you must seek out ways to do it—not your boss, not your employer, but you must do it.

During Daniel's career, he could have been overwhelmed by the myriad of things involved in learning a new language, new customs, and new methods for doing things. And yet, his attitude seemed to be that he would take on the challenge and learn everything he needed to know to be the best that he could be at his job. Recognizing that having the desire to learn and having the aptitude to learn are two different things, we have the assurance, as Daniel did, that God is able to help us in areas where we may be lacking. Isn't it marvelous to know that we have a Helper who will not only teach us all things but will also give us wisdom to seek resources and opportunities to expand our knowledge and to learn ways to improve our skills while enhancing our capabilities? Just as in the days of Daniel, we know that God is the One who gives wisdom and knowledge, and we need only go first to Him, and He will direct us in any new learning venture.

But what happens when we are eager to learn something new and different and yet we are faced with the tedious sameness of our every day jobs? Is there a way to break out into something new? My friend Rita did exactly that. She had worked in the wire-transfer area of the local bank for a number of years. She was really looking for a new challenge and began searching for new opportunities on her company's job posting board. After several weeks, she identified a position in the accounting department, which she believed would be perfect for her. She applied for the position and later discovered that one of her very best friends had also applied. Her friend was ultimately hired for the position, leaving Rita very disappointed. She describes that time in her life this way:

> I had prayed for this new position and just knew the Lord wanted me to have it. I couldn't understand why He had allowed my friend to get the job instead of me. My biggest question was, "Why?"
>
> A few days later, the personnel director contacted me to see if I would like to be his new assistant (the job my friend had vacated). I had no experience in human resources, but after praying about it, I decided to give it a try. Two months after joining the department, the assistant personnel director quit, and I was promoted to the job. During that time, I was able to learn many new things, and ultimately (a few years later), I became the personnel director.
>
> While my friend enjoyed a good career in accounting, the accounting department was consolidated and moved to another city. As a result, she had to take a less interesting job in the commercial banking division. Meanwhile, my job was growing by leaps and bounds. I inherited two other cities with personnel issues to manage, then later, five more cities, and I eventually became the human resources consultant to 36 banking centers around the state. I began to travel a lot, meet wonderful people, and learn many new things.
>
> God certainly knew what He was doing. He knew that the position I wanted so badly would ultimately be eliminated and would not provide the new experience I was seeking. But the job that He provided allowed me to grow in ways I never dreamed of, while allowing me the privilege of traveling, meeting new

people, and making lifelong friends. If God had answered my prayer the way I wanted Him to answer it, I would have been out of a job or doing work that wasn't nearly as challenging. However, He allowed me to see that His will is always far better than I ever could have hoped.

A terrific lesson to learn: God's will is always far better than any of us could ever hope. But what I especially enjoyed about my friend's experience was that her heart's desire was to continue to learn and to grow. Being completely aware of that desire—and I suspect He placed it in her heart—God created an avenue where that desire could be realized. By not answering her prayer in the way that she imagined, but instead answering it in a way that accomplished what she yearned for, God caused my friend to grow exponentially. Not only did she learn about an entirely different department of her company and what she was capable of doing, but also, and more importantly, she learned of another aspect of the character of God: He is the ultimate teacher.

As we go about our daily jobs building our skills in our professions or even developing our talents for an entirely new career, we will learn more about ourselves and more about our Creator. Just as with Daniel, we will begin to know that when we rely on God to increase our learning potential, not only will we achieve career satisfaction, but we will learn that each new experience teaches us more about trusting Him.

Chapter Ten

Principle 5—Seek Out Mentors

Faith at Work Tip: Admitting that you need help is the first step to obtaining it

Let us therefore come boldly to the throne of grace, that we may obtain mercy and find grace to help in time of need (Hebrews 4:16).

Once upon a time, early in her career before she knew anything at all about the importance of not making unnecessary enemies at work, Janice offended a very important woman in her company, Linda. She didn't mean to offend Linda, but somehow she got on the other woman's wrong side, and she was a formidable enemy to have. Linda was well thought of in the company and was responsible for one of the most productive business units in the firm. As a result, she had certain privileges that allowed her to bend the rules to suit her needs, and no one seemed to have a problem with it—no one except Janice. As she began to notice some of the shortcuts that Linda was taking, she innocently mentioned it to Linda's boss. Of course, this piece of information made its way back to Linda, and she was livid. She declared war on Janice.

Janice was befuddled. She wasn't quite sure what to do to make things right with Linda, and the work environment was becoming unbearable. Fortunately for Janice, there was a senior manager named Maggie in the firm who had observed the entire situation. Maggie thought Janice had a lot of potential but that she lacked the necessary savvy to navigate her way through the shark-invested waters at the firm. Maggie had a great relationship with both Linda and Janice, and she took it upon herself to become the peacemaker. She invited them both out after work one day and had a casual impromptu meeting to resolve the conflict. Maggie used the time to mediate the misunderstanding, and by the end of the meeting, Linda and Janice had agreed to give each other a second chance and to start over. To this day, Janice remains grateful to Maggie for reaching out to help her. Janice related, "If it weren't for Maggie, I would have sloshed my way around that company like a bull in a china shop. I have her to thank for teaching me how to handle delicate situations, as well as how to win friends and influence people."

Couldn't we all use a helping hand like the one Maggie provided? Wouldn't we all like to have someone who is interested in how we are doing at work and who is willing to teach us how to do things even better? Janice was fortunate to have Maggie help her through a tough spot. Janice's relationship with Linda might have continued to deteriorate if Maggie hadn't invested herself and her time to help Linda and Janice reconcile their differences with each other. Maggie also used her influence as a senior manager of the firm to give credibility to each person. The mere fact that she thought of both of them as being important enough to want to help them immediately caused them to view each other differently. This leads us to our fifth principle to seek out others who are willing to help you.

In Janice's case, it wasn't necessary for her to seek out help; Maggie willingly offered her assistance. But what if Maggie hadn't come along? How long would the dispute between Linda and Janice have festered? At some point, it would have been important for Janice to discover this important principle, which has helped many people in the workplace succeed. We are not islands and are not able to figure it all out on our own. We need other people, and other people need us.

When Daniel found himself in a tough spot and needed to know what his boss, the king, had dreamed, he immediately requested the assistance of his three closest colleagues: Shadrach, Meshach, and Abednego (Daniel 2:17-18). He knew that if he was not able to decipher the dream, he and his co-workers would be killed. As people of faith, we will often find ourselves in some very tough spots at work. And while God is always our source, He often uses other people to strengthen and aid us. We should be on the lookout for them because they are out there, and they are more than willing to help in most instances. One of the ways we can get the help that we need to be more successful at work is to find a mentor. A mentor can be an invaluable resource in helping us to navigate through all sorts of tough spots and can assist us in our professional development.

What, exactly, is a mentor? A mentor can best be described as a professional helper. A mentor is usually someone who has more experience than we do and who is usually at a higher level within the organization. They are typically people who know the rules of the workplace—the written rules as well as the unwritten ones. Mentors are colleagues who can help us to develop professionally, and who may even have the power to give us the additional exposure that we need to become more effective in our work. They can be helpful in a number of different ways, but primarily they do the following:

- Provide **coaching**—as workplace situations arise, they can coach you on the best way to handle them
- Provide **networking opportunities**—they can expose you to the people that you need to know in the organization
- Provide **career counseling**—as you make important decisions regarding your career, they can assist in guiding you in identifying your career goals and aspirations
- Provide **skills development**—their support can be helpful in developing or enhancing the skill sets you will need to meet the needs and objectives of the organization

Why Have a Mentor?

As much as we would like to think that we have it all figured out, many of our workplace problems surface because we don't. As a result, there are many benefits to having a mentor. Throughout my career, I have had both formal and informal mentors. The lessons that I learned from them, in many cases, would have been missed opportunities without their involvement. They have increased my organizational awareness by telling me the unwritten rules. Remember the story about the red shoes in chapter one? Needless to say, I didn't have a mentor at that time and, therefore, no one to coach me on the merits of wearing black pumps as opposed to wearing red stilettos! It's simple information such as that, which can help you to navigate through the organization in large and small matters. Having a mentor can give you access to contacts in different areas of the organization. This can be extremely important if you work for a larger employer. As you attempt to get things done, you will often need the aid of members of various departments, and a mentor may be able to introduce you to the people who can help you the most. A mentor can also share their knowledge and experiences so that you gain insight about what is important in your organization. They can be invaluable resources to help you strategize about your career objectives and to help you develop critical skills you will need to grow professionally.

Finding a Mentor

You may be wondering about the best way to find a mentor. If your organization doesn't have a formal mentoring program, don't lose heart. You can take the initiative to locate a mentor yourself. Start by looking around your organization to determine those who have been successful in it. Focus on those who may be in a field similar to your own or who work in a profession that you would like to learn more about. A mentor can be someone who is either inside or outside your organization. Obviously, having one inside the organization may be more beneficial because they may know many of the players you will be interacting with. However, having a mentor outside the organization has its benefits as well. Someone who is not a part of your organization may give you a fresh perspective or a different way of looking at things. They may also be able to help you see your organization from the outside looking in, which is an important capability to have.

Identify the benefits that each potential mentor can provide, as well as any potential challenges. Consider those who can help you achieve the goals you have set for yourself. Think carefully about what type of characteristics you want your mentor to possess. For example, do you want them to have strong listening skills? Do you prefer someone who is very direct, or someone who has a softer approach? Is it important that they be outgoing by nature, or that they be relaxed and easy-going? Also examine the areas in which you want your mentor to be able to provide insight. Are you interested in gaining insight about technical skills or leadership skills? Do you want guidance on work/life balance or suggestions for networking? As you consider all of this, create a list of all possible mentors, and then evaluate them against the characteristics you desire to determine your top choice. But above all, pray and ask God to guide you in selecting a mentor to help you.

Once you have identified some potential mentors, schedule a meeting with your first choice to begin the recruiting process. Since you will be approaching her, you will need to be able to articulate why it makes sense for her to mentor you. Besides giving her an opportunity to find out what a fabulous person you are, you may also want to share specific benefits she will realize as a mentor:

- The potential to gain access to new ideas and perspectives
- Getting direct exposure to obstacles encountered by employees at different levels in the organization
- Enhancing own career growth and the success of the organization by sharing in the development of a junior colleague
- Enhancing organizational communication

In most instances, people are flattered to be identified as potential mentors because it signifies that they are people whom others look up too, and this can be irresistible.

What Happens Next?

Once you have gained a commitment from a mentor, be prepared to discuss expectations from the relationship. Remember, it is your job to manage your own development. You should be able to define the goals for your participation by considering the best way to utilize your mentor's perspective and the resources they make available to you. It is up to you not only to create a personal development plan but also to act on it. Share your development needs and concerns with your mentor, and ask them for suggestions or advice to help you improve. Naturally, when asking for advice, you must be willing to receive constructive feedback and to share your progress with your mentor.

It will take time and effort to build your mentoring relationship, but there are ways to make sure that you are experiencing the full benefits of the relationship.

1. Establish a regular meeting time and always be prepared for the meetings.

2.   Have an agenda for your meetings with your mentor. Don't make the mistake of just meeting to meet. Remember, your mentor is providing you with a very valuable resource—her time—you don't want to waste it.

3.   Build trust by never disclosing confidential information that the mentor may share with you.

4.   Establish goals for the relationship, as well as goals for your development, and review them periodically to determine progress.

5.   Stay focused on your development needs, and don't be afraid to ask for your mentor's help if they are in a position to work with you on skills that you need to develop.

6.   Be committed to the relationship. Make sure that you understand what your mentor expects from you and do it.

Finding a mentor is one way of seeking others to help you. Another way is to identify a prayer partner. Prayer partners are people who commit themselves to praying about issues that you are addressing at work. Prayer partners need not be associated with your organization; in fact, in many cases it may be better if they are not. However, having a prayer partner who is also a colleague in your office can have significant value as well. Your prayer partner should be someone whom you trust completely. She needs to be someone who is also a committed believer in Jesus Christ and someone who has a strong relationship with Him.

When seeking out a prayer partner, do something that is very obvious—pray. Ask God for guidance in identifying the person whom you should partner with in prayer. You want to look for someone who has these characteristics:

- Ability to keep confidences—the last thing you need or want is someone who takes your prayer needs and shares them with someone else.
- Spiritual maturity—this person needs to understand the spiritual battles that exist in the workplace as well as the emotional and physical battles that are often more obvious.
- Committed to the process—you will find many people who say they will be praying for you, and yet, never do. Or if they do, it is cursory at best. You need someone who digs into the process, who

takes the commitment seriously, and whom you can know is truly praying about the issues that you bring to them.

- Accountable—this will go both ways. A prayer partner must be someone who is willing to be accountable to you and God for petitioning in prayer on your behalf. Likewise, you must be accountable to them to share the truth, the total situation, and the ultimate outcomes of your prayer request.
- Friendship—someone you know well. You want to be sure of the intent of their heart, and discovering this may take some time as your friendship develops.

As you begin thinking of people who have these characteristics, make a list of how each person demonstrates these characteristics in their day-to-day lives. Some common traits that you should see demonstrated consistently by them are their love for others, joy in spite of circumstances, peace and serenity, patience, kindness, goodness, and faithfulness—each of which represent the gifts from God that true people of faith will have.

Once you have prayed about your potential partner and know whom you should approach, talk with them about it, and share with them your desire to have them as a partner in prayer. Be prepared to describe how you think this will benefit the workplace and how it will benefit you. Be willing to make the arrangement reciprocal and offer to pray about issues of concern for them. Finally, tell them to pray about the decision to become your partner. It is an important decision to make, and you want to be sure that they have also sought God's guidance before making it.

After a commitment is made, agree on the process. When will you meet? Will you pray together, apart, or both? How long is your partnership intended to last? Will it last until one of you leaves the company, or until you both feel it is no longer serving its purpose? These are all the things you should settle at the beginning so that both of you know what is expected. This may feel a bit formal at first, but it underscores the seriousness of becoming someone's prayer partner. Prayer is important business, and having someone pray with you is powerful. Be clear on the issues that are most important to you as they relate to your workplace. After all, you are joining with another person to approach the throne of God. Get a mental image of that in your mind and remind yourself of the scripture that says, "The prayer of a person living right with God is something powerful to be reckoned with." (James 5:16— *The Message*) Or as the Amplified translation says, "The earnest (heart-felt, continued) prayer of a righteous man makes tremendous power available [dynamic in its working]." Since this is true for one person, imagine how much more powerful it can be for two.

The truth is we all need power in our workplace: power to get along with others, power to do difficult tasks, power to be successful at work. Learning to ask for help when it is needed is a way to move towards that success which God desires for all of us to experience while at work. Don't be afraid to ask for it, whether through mentoring or through prayer. The relationships that can be built in both partnerships can develop into lifelong friendships. Daniel was aware of this principle and used it often. As a result, he experienced many successes in his career. As you begin to grasp the power of this principle and to use it, you will be amazed to see the success that is waiting just for you.

Chapter Eleven

Principle 6—Be Punctual, Prepared, and Positive

Faith at Work Tip: You can choose to be on time, prepared and have a great attitude

But I discipline my body and bring it into subjection, lest, when I have preached to others I myself should become disqualified (1 Corinthians 9:27).

As the elevator doors opened, Becky looked quickly from left to right to see if anyone was in the hallway, before stepping out. Whew! No one from her office had seen her, yet. She couldn't afford to be late again. Becky was finding the hours of her new job extremely challenging. Her boss actually expected her to be at work promptly at eight, and she was not adapting well at all. She had already been chewed out by her boss for having been habitually late. If she was fortunate, she just might be able to make it all the way to her desk without anyone noticing that she was 15 minutes late again. She had a good plan too. She would drop off her briefcase in the storage closet, go quickly to the break room and grab a cup of coffee, and then walk casually to her desk as though she had been there all along. By the time she got her computer up and running and spread a few papers across her desk, she could go back to the storage closet, retrieve her briefcase, and she would be home free.

The plan worked like a charm. She was secretly congratulating herself and thinking how clever she was when her colleague Bob came by her desk and said, "Hey, Becky, where have you been? The boss was

looking for you earlier for a meeting that started twenty minutes ago."
Oh-oh! So that was where everyone was—at a meeting she had completely forgotten about. And even worse, she wasn't prepared to update her boss on their marketing campaign.

Does this sound familiar? Have you ever had a day like Becky's where everything seemed to go wrong? And to complicate matters even further, have you ever tried to manipulate the situation to avoid being accountable, the way Becky did? It's probably safe to say that we have all had our share of days when our tactics were questionable and clearly not a demonstration of our beliefs. And like Becky, some of us may even wonder at times why God allowed so many early birds to be the boss over so many of us night owls. What may seem like the easiest principle of all to keep can be one of the most challenging to those of us who believe the work day really shouldn't start until after noon.

Truthfully, Principle 6—being punctual, prepared, and positive—may indeed be the one that we personally have the most control over. Think about it, the other principles we have discussed so far may have a lot of components to them that we cannot easily control. For example, your talents are gifts that you are born with, and although you may be able to do something to keep developing your talents, you had to start with the gift in the first place. You had no control over how you got it or why you have it. But being on time, being prepared, and being positive are all things that you can choose. Granted, it may be easier for early birds to make it to work on time, but it doesn't mean that we night owls can't develop the habit as well. And this applies not only to arriving at work but also to being on time with assignments and for appointments all throughout the day.

This principle is one avenue we can pursue for career success because it reflects how we value others. Have you ever sat in a meeting when there was no agenda, people arrived late, the meeting seemed to have no purpose, and it lasted forever? How did this make you feel? You probably began to feel as though your time had been wasted. The thought might have even occurred to you that the meeting probably would probably have been conducted a lot differently if the president of the firm had attended. And in fact, you would probably be right. You would come away from that experience feeling that you had not been valued as a person.

From a godly perspective Principle 6, also known as "the three P's," is important to our career success because it reminds us to put others first. When we arrive on time for appointments with others, we are saying, "I value you and your time." When we are prepared for meetings or other scheduled events, it says to others, "I think you are important enough to receive my best effort." And when we maintain a positive attitude, others are naturally attracted to us because people prefer being around people who view the glass as half full rather than half empty. Think about those people whom you most enjoy being with. More than likely, they have a positive outlook on life and are always looking for the best in a situation, rather than the worst.

But first things first, how do we develop the three P's in our life? It starts with the same focus of mind that Daniel had. Remember Daniel purposed in his heart those things that he would tolerate in his life and those things that he would not. He decided very early on what type of employee he was going to be. Once he made that decision, he set about putting a plan into action. Once the plan was in place, he acted on it. The same kind of thoughtfulness needs to be a part of developing the three P's.

Being Punctual

If we want to be punctual, this could be a matter of time management. I remember a particularly funny episode of one of my favorite sitcoms, *I Love Lucy*. Lucy had a problem with being on time and decided to solve the problem by changing the clocks in her home to give herself some extra time. Unfortunately, she turned all the clocks back one hour rather than forward one hour. Not recognizing her mistake, she proceeded to get ready for a very important business dinner with her new system of time management in place. Thinking that she had an extra hour, she took her time getting ready. It wasn't until her husband, Ricky, noticed that it was getting extremely dark outside despite the early hour showing on the clock, that the error was discovered. Needless to say, they ended up being an hour late for their dinner engagement, rather than on time as they had planned. Lucy had purposed in her heart to be on time, but the plan she put into action was the wrong one.

It's easy to see why having the right plan to manage your time can be critical. Let's examine some of the root causes for not being punctual.

I. **Organizational Skills**

Having poor organizational skills can frequently be the culprit when people find themselves struggling to get their assignments in on time. If you know that you waste a lot of time due to a tendency of being disorganized, then you may need some help to better organize yourself so that more time isn't wasted. This could result in the need to take a time management workshop, or it might mean having a person who is organized help you to develop a system that is going to keep you on track. Think about what works best for you. If you are the kind of person who works better with lists, then develop a list of things that you need to get done each day and allow it to be your guide. Or if you have a major project that's due, break it down into smaller pieces so that you can determine the amount of time it will take for each part to get done before committing to a deadline that may be unreasonable. As you become more organized, you will understand how you are using your time and you will begin to use it more wisely.

2. **Use of Calendar**

Sometimes, the reason that we find ourselves constantly late is because we don't use our calendars in a way that will benefit us or because we don't have a calendar at all. If you are a busy person, then you need to have a way to track your time. Whether you use an electronic calendar or a paper one, it's important that you maintain some record of your appointments, project deadlines, and other important matters that take up time during the day. In addition, be sure to allow enough time for the activity being placed on your calendar. If you underestimate how long something is actually going to take you to do, you will find yourself running late all day long. For example, for years I went to a hair stylist who was constantly late. I couldn't figure it out because everyone had an appointment time, but she could never stay on schedule. Needless to say, I became very frustrated and ultimately changed stylists. My new stylist was very punctual. Although she had more customers then my prior stylist, she was still able to remain on schedule. One day, I asked her how she was able to do it. She replied that she not only scheduled the person on her calendar but also scheduled the service they would be having. She went on to say that she knew it took longer to apply a perm on someone's hair then to merely give a haircut. If her customer wanted a perm, then she would allow 30 minutes on her calendar, but if they wanted a haircut, she would allow 15 minutes. By doing this, she was always able to stay on time.

Another important tip for managing your calendar is not to allow others to use your time inappropriately. If you know that you have a very busy day and your calendar is already jammed with things to do, you will need to be very disciplined about not allowing someone to stop by your desk or office to talk. Instead, you may have to say, "I'm really busy right now, but I would love to catch up with you. Why don't we schedule lunch?" Remember, you must keep a tight rein on your calendar, or you will wonder why, at the end of the day, you are still running behind.

I actually maintain more than one calendar—a professional one and a personal one. Of course, this can be time consuming because I must track my time on two different calendars, but I've gotten into the habit of looking at both of them and coordinating my time appropriately. You may be able to do this just as successfully with one calendar. Again, the principle theme is whatever works for you.

3. Being Prepared

You may be on time, but what happens when you get there? Are you prepared? That's the question we should always ask ourselves each day at work. Obviously, some of us have spent many years being trained to do the work that we do. That's a big picture issue. What we are talking about now goes into the details. Are you prepared to make that presentation? Have you prepared for that sales call you must make today? Did you prepare the conference room for that meeting your boss is hosting? Are you prepared?

One of my favorite mentors was also one of the best I've ever seen at being prepared. No matter what she was asked to do, Margaret was always ready to do it. She had an uncanny knack of knowing exactly what her boss wanted and always giving a little extra without being asked. Her presentations were always over the top because of her preparedness. She worked long hours to make sure that she was thorough, accurate, and that the information she was providing was insightful. Needless to say, she experienced a lot of career success, because she truly understood what it meant to be prepared. She did not procrastinate, and she was always innovative with her approach to getting things done.

When we look at the life of Daniel, we see some of the same qualities exhibited in his work style. He was always prepared. He made sure that everything he did was well thought out, and he made a point of being better prepared than his colleagues, which led to a lot of his success. More importantly, his prayer life kept him focused on what was most important and on putting first things first. As a result, he didn't waste time on nonessential things, but instead put his energy into getting the most out of his work day.

Being prepared means being ready for any possibility. I will never forget a time when I was to make a big presentation to a room full of senior managers of my firm. I spent many days preparing the presentation and had included many charts and graphs on Powerpoint to provide a visual image of my key points. As I was making some final changes to the presentation, the thought occurred to me that I should be extra familiar with the slides so that I didn't have to constantly refer to my notes while speaking. As a result, I practically memorized every slide and my notes for each one. At the time, I thought this was probably overdoing it, but I decided to practice the presentation in the mirror several times as well.

Little did I know how much that preparation time was going to be needed. As I was about to come to the podium to give my presentation, one of the administrative assistants accidentally turned off the laptop that had my slide presentation on it. When I noticed that there were no slides on the overhead projector, I almost panicked, thinking there was no way I could do the presentation without those slides. It soon became apparent that it was going to take a few minutes for the laptop to reboot, and in the meantime, there I stood with all eyes on me waiting for my presentation to begin. It suddenly occurred to me that I knew the material. I had prepared extensively, and every aspect of that presentation was as well known to me as the color of my hair. And so I proceeded to give the presentation without any slides and without any notes. When the slides finally did appear midway through the presentation, I was able to pick right up where I had left off, as though the slides had been there all along. I would not have been able to do that had I not taken the extra time to be prepared for the unexpected.

I believe that so often when we have experiences like that, we look back at them and realize that it was God that caused us to go above and beyond our normal limitations. I remembering thinking afterwards when many colleagues came to congratulate me on my presentation, that it was God who had placed it in my heart and mind to over-prepare. He already knew what was going to be required and that circumstances would exist that would require the extra effort. It also taught me the important lesson of being prepared in season and out of season, because you never know when you will need to go above and beyond what would typically be expected of you.

Being Positive

If anyone were to describe Renea in one word, they would say "laughter." I have worked with Renea for many years, and her laughter and positive attitude are infectious. You can't be around her for very long before you are laughing and smiling too. As a result, everyone enjoys being around Renea. In fact, when most people are feeling down, they can count on her to lift their spirits. If you were to ask Renea how she manages to always have such an upbeat, positive attitude, she would tell you that she has a lot to be thankful for. It's not because she hasn't had her own share of tough times, it's simply because she chooses to see all the good things in her life and to be happy about it.

That was the essence of Daniel's character, too. Daniel had been taken from his home at an early age and placed into forced labor. He was made to learn a culture that was very different from his own and was constantly having to defend his beliefs to people who believed quite differently than he did. Despite all this, he chose to be positive. You will never read of Daniel being anything but positive, approachable, and seeing life as full of possibilities. He didn't allow his personal circumstances to affect his work. Instead he worked harder than his contemporaries did and rose to a very high level within the organization. He never allowed himself the luxury of a pity party, but instead trusted in the sovereignty of God and went about living his faith at work where all his co-workers could see it demonstrated daily.

As people of faith, our attitudes should reflect what we believe in. No matter what the circumstances, we have an opportunity to demonstrate our confidence in God's sovereignty by displaying a positive attitude. If things aren't going well at work, we can be examples of how to deal with difficulties and challenges in a positive manner. People should recognize a difference in the way we operate and in the way we handle disappointments. Likewise, we should be there to encourage others who may struggle in this area. If you know someone who is constantly negative or has a tendency to be critical, it provides an opportunity to model behavior that can be more uplifting and that reflects a different way to view the world.

Our ability to do this will largely depend on how much time we spend in God's presence reading His Word and meditating on scriptures that will give us the different outlook we need. It is only as we change our thinking that we can begin to change our attitudes. Our thinking can only be changed as we become better acquainted with God and His character, and develop a trusting relationship with Him.

Practicing being punctual, being prepared, and being positive may seem quite basic at first. But it is when we go back to basics that we can begin to see changes in our lives and in how others perceive us. Remember, you have control over the three P's. You can choose to develop the habits of being on time, being ready, and staying positive, or you can choose not to. However, if you master this very simple principle, you will be amazed at the changes in yourself and the changes others will see in you.

Chapter Twelve

Principle 7—Maintain Your Purpose

Faith at Work Tip: The purpose God has for your life is better than anything you can imagine

And we know that all things work together for good to those who love God, to those who are the called according to His purpose (Romans 8:28).

The final principle to career success is one that many of us will have to learn the hard way. In fact, initially upon reading the chapter title you may have wondered why you would want to run from your purpose. That is a good question. The truth is that we all have dreams and goals. I like to think that God places dreams in our hearts as a path to serve Him and others. However, some of us will never realize those dreams until we realize a very important truth: God's ways of fulfilling those dreams may be very different from how we would fulfill our dreams if everything were left solely up to us.

What do I mean by this? Let's take a look at the story of Joseph. Joseph was known as a dreamer because he not only had great dreams for his life but he also had a talent for interpreting others' dreams as well. When Joseph was still a teenager, he dreamt that he would one day be the boss over many people. In fact, his dream was so vivid that he knew with certainty that not only would he be at the top of his game from a career perspective, but he would also be the most successful member of his family. He was the youngest of eleven brothers, and frankly, he was delighted to know that, some day, his older brothers were going to have to answer to him. Because he thought this was such great news, he decided to share his dream with his brothers.

Needless to say, his brothers were nowhere near as enthusiastic about this dream as Joseph was. In fact, it made them downright angry. They began to plot for a way to get rid of Joseph, and after a time, were successful in selling him into slavery. This seems rather drastic to our way of thinking, and I'm sure poor Joseph didn't appreciate the turn of events either. Joseph ended up far away from home, working for one of the local officials in an entirely different country. Things were going well for a while, but through a terrible set of circumstances, Joseph was falsely accused of a crime he didn't commit and landed in prison. He remained in prison for several years with no chance for an appeal.

One day, two men were also thrown into jail with him, and he befriended them. Both of these men had come out of positions that allowed them access to the most powerful ruler in the country. As it so happened, both men had dreams one night, but neither of them knew what the dreams meant. Since dream interpretation was a divine gift that Joseph had, he correctly interpreted both men's dreams. In one case, one of the men was soon to be freed from prison, and Joseph pleaded for him to help him get out of prison once he was free. Although the man had good intentions, he ultimately forgot all about Joseph, so Joseph remained in prison for several more years.

If you are familiar with this story, you know that everything ultimately worked out for Joseph. Not only was he eventually freed from prison but he was also ultimately promoted to a position second only to the king. He was responsible for the entire government and eventually was reunited with his family during a terrible famine when his brothers came looking for food. Ultimately, the dream that he had for his life while he was a young boy came true, but clearly the method used to realize the dream was very different than the way he might have imagined it.

Imagine if you had been Joseph with this big dream for your life. Can't you see yourself wondering what in heaven's name was going on throughout the 17 years that it took for the dream to finally be realized? Surely, when he was sold into slavery he must have wondered whether it had been a dream or just his imagination. And when he was falsely accused and thrown into prison, can't you imagine him saying, "God, how could this have happened? I'm innocent." And certainly after many years, he must have been discouraged and might even have begun to doubt that the dream he had so long ago had been real. He definitely didn't want to remain in his circumstances; he begged the other prisoner to help him get out. Like many of us, Joseph might have been thinking that his circumstances couldn't be a part of his purpose. After all, wasn't he supposed to be the boss over all?

Since we have read the end of the story, we know that, indeed, every single circumstance, every job he was given, and every place that he landed, were all a part of readying Joseph for his ultimate purpose. Even when he made an attempt to get out of his circumstances, he couldn't do so because the purpose that he was destined to fulfill included a test of his faith. What does this tell us? Many times, as our dreams grow dimmer over the years, we, too, may begin to wonder how our current circumstances—our present job, our current boss, our career, our employer—are remotely connected with what we might have thought we were supposed to be doing in life. We look around us and say, "This can't be right, my purpose isn't this, I'm supposed to be doing _____." However we may fill in the blank, the result is the same. We come to a crossroad that is a test of faith when the dream we believe God placed in our hearts doesn't line up with our current situation. For many of us, that is when we begin to run from our purpose and sabotage our career success.

The subtle truth is that we are often unaware that we are actually running from our purpose. We may even talk ourselves into believing that we are actually running toward it. This is how it works: We have an idea of what our dream job or dream career is supposed to be, and we then proceed to do everything that is humanly possible to achieve it. Of course, some glitch always gets in the way, and we work hard to either remove the glitch or to get around it. But then, some other barrier pops up, and we do our best to beat it down or push it aside, all the while using up years of energy, emotion, knowledge and power to get this dream to work out our way. But when it doesn't, we become frustrated, and we wonder what else we need to do to move our career along. We toil and toil and may have a few successes, but even those aren't what we thought they would be. The months and years go by until we finally stop, look up into the heavens, and ask, "God what am I doing wrong to fulfill the dream that you placed in my heart?"

The answer to that question is in the question itself. We ask, "What am I doing?" rather than asking, "God, what do You want to do to fulfill the dream you have placed in my heart?" It may be that God's purpose for you is to go through the exact experiences that you are going through—to work at the company you are working, for the boss you are working for, with the colleagues that you are working with, doing the job you are employed to do. If you're like me, you may be shaking your head right now thinking that this can't be right, that you are supposed to be doing _____. But remember, the path you are on may be leading you to the dream you so desire; however, it may not look like the path that you imagined would get you there.

I recall a specific time in my life when I was sure the path I was headed down was on the opposite side of the universe from where I was supposed to be. You see, I have known for some time that I would be a writer. I have kept journals and diaries from the time I was a small child. I love the written word. I love to read and I love to write. I even attempted to write a book when I was a teenager, but never quite finished it. As time went by, I eventually put the dream of writing aside to focus on finishing college, starting a career, and ultimately, having a family, but the dream was never far from my heart.

After many years had passed, an idea for a book began to percolate in my mind. I started working on the manuscript in my spare time, and after a couple of years, I had a draft ready to present to a publisher. Wonder of wonders, the book was published and I was over the moon. I begin thinking that my career as a writer was taking off and that I would be checking out of the corporate scene and moving on with God's purpose for my life. Oh, happy day! The funny thing was that it didn't work out exactly that way. As most writers will tell you, there are millions of books on the market and just as many writers. So, being able to quit your day job after writing your first book is not always an option financially, as I was soon to find out.

At the time my book was published, I became very busy at my day job. I thought that all God had to do was cause everyone to want to buy my book, and then I could quit my job and begin to write full time and start fulfilling His purpose for my life. I waited with such anticipation, just knowing that God and I were on the same page. After all, hadn't He placed in my heart the dream to become a writer? Since it was His idea, I could do nothing but succeed—right? Well, not exactly. It began to dawn on me that God and I were on the same page as far as the dream He had placed in my heart, but I had completely missed the boat when it came to understanding how He was going to fulfill that dream in my life.

But before I came to that realization, I decided to help God out a bit. About that same time, the firm I was working for was sold to another company. Unlike everyone else, who was stunned and shocked, I was rejoicing! I just knew that I would receive a huge separation package with benefits, and it would be the cushion I needed to start my writing career. I believed that to be God's plan for me. While everyone else was doing everything they could to stay employed, I was doing everything I could to get a severance package. I went about praising God and thanking Him for this splendid turn of events. When my new boss called me to discuss my department, I was the most gracious person on the earth, assuring him that I would do everything I could before my departure to assist him in taking over my area. He seemed puzzled and even said, "You act as though you are going somewhere." That was my first inkling that the plan wasn't going to go exactly the way I had hoped it would. But I shrugged it off, thinking that surely he couldn't be thinking about keeping me there. After all, God's purpose for me was to be a full-time writer.

Some time passed, and I received a visit from my new boss. I was so excited! I knew he would be discussing the terms of my separation and notifying me about my final day with the firm. As I sat opposite him, we both smiled pleasantly. It was then that he dropped the bomb. He began by telling me that he was pleased to offer me a new job with great benefits, earning a really nice salary. At first, I couldn't hear the words that he was saying. I had been busy calculating my severance in my mind, so the offer of continued employment was getting lost in the conversation I was having in my head. I even heard myself saying that another colleague would probably be better suited for that particular job. But he insisted that I was perfect for it. I couldn't believe it! I needed that severance! I wanted that severance! I was relying on that severance! My purpose was to be a writer!

A few days later, after I regained consciousness from the fog I had been in, I realized that I was still employed in a job I didn't want, stuck in a career I wanted to bail out of while simultaneously running from

God's ultimate purpose for me. I knew this because I know the sovereignty of God. It was no surprise to Him that I was offered a job that others would have died for. It was no surprise to Him that I was bound and determined to have His purpose for my life fulfilled my way. And it was no surprise to Him that I would ultimately stop running long enough to ask, "God, what do you want to do to fulfill the dream You have placed in my heart?"

And so, I began to realize that I had to stop running from my purpose and step into each circumstance with the confidence that, despite how it might look, my journey, with all its twists and turns, would still end with the dream being fulfilled. It changed how I did the job that I didn't want. I became a better employee because I began to see it as an integral part of my purpose. Each day (and believe me there were some tough days), I would say to myself, "This job has been provided so that I can be a better writer some day. The experiences that I will have on this job, the people I will meet, and the trials and successes I will experience are all a part of God's purpose for me, and I will embrace each one."

How does this fit in with career success? When we begin to see our present circumstances as divinely planned by God, we approach those circumstances differently. You may be in a position today that isn't the exact job that you want to spend your life doing. That's OK. However, don't make everyone around you suffer by being bitter or having a negative attitude simply because you believe that you are supposed to be doing something else. Instead, accept the fact that there are aspects to your job that may prove in the years ahead to have been very valuable to you. Are you learning to be more detailed? Is it a chance to become better at building relationships? Or maybe you have a need to learn patience to wait on God's timing. No matter what the situation may be, it's all for your good. Stop running from what can be used by God to prepare you for His purpose for your life.

Jesus did not enter into full-time ministry until He was 30 years old. However, from the very beginning, He knew what God's purpose was for His life. While on a trip with his parents when He was only 12 years old, He was unknowingly left behind because he had been busy teaching and discussing deep spiritual matters with the leaders of His time. I'm sure that part of Him was anxious to get started with the purpose for His life. However, when His mother questioned Him about why He had remained behind to talk when it was time to return home, He dutifully returned with His family and began learning the skills of a carpenter. It would have been easy for Him to ask, "What on earth am I going to need to know how to do this for?" But instead, He became an expert carpenter and worked diligently serving His customers until it was time for His ministry to begin.

Who knows how many things he learned as a carpenter were ultimately valuable for him to know during His short yet powerful ministry on earth? We can only imagine that in any type of craftsman role, one would have to be accustomed to being very precise, to listen carefully to what the customer wanted, and to be able to make those items to the customer's specification. We can imagine Jesus building relationships with people during this time as He worked alongside them. And clearly, He would have had to develop the skill of listening to others so that He could understand the best way to meet their needs. Even though the Bible is silent on those years, we know that in everything He did, He continued to please God and have favor with the people around Him. So we must assume that He didn't spend any of his time complaining about working as a carpenter when He was meant to be the Savior of the world.

The same could be said about Daniel. He was taken far from home and taken to a place that was unlike anything he had ever known or dreamed about. He could have spent his time thinking of ways to get back to where he thought he was supposed to be. Instead, he accepted the sovereignty of God and looked at his circumstances and the job that he was hired for as an opportunity to pursue his purpose. He probably didn't know how all the pieces fit together as he was working day by day, but he trusted that he was exactly where he needed to be to fulfill the purpose only he was destined to fulfill.

What about you? Are you viewing your current position as a part of God's plan for your life at this time? Or are you still debating whether it could possibly be something that escaped God's attention? One of the best truths every written is found in Romans 8:28, "And we know that all things work together for good to them that love God, to them who are the called according to his purpose." This tells us that when we are in a relationship with God, He calls us to something specific that is meeting a specific purpose. It also tells us that everything will work together for good. This doesn't mean that each single event will look good to us. Each job that we have may not in and of itself seem good to us. But what we are assured of is the fact that at the end of the day, when it's all said and done, everything will work out for good. Not only will it work out for our good but also for the good of anyone else whom God chooses to involve who are also called according to His purpose.

What this also points out is that it's not all about us. Instead, it's all about God. How He wants to use our lives and our jobs or careers will be a blessing to us, but it will also be a blessing to others, as well. Think as if you were viewing a really great classic film and in the middle of it the main character began to go through some difficulties; you wouldn't jump up, leave the movie, and say, "I have seen enough, this movie isn't going the way I think it should." No, it's more likely that you would stay glued to your seat, wondering how on earth the character was going to get through that plot twist, and remain until you saw how it all worked out. Well the truth of the matter is that we don't have a choice when it comes to the purpose God has planned for us. We may try to run from it, and we may think we have even succeeded for a while, but all we will have really done is taken the scenic route to the place God wants us to be. And it will be the place we will want to be once we get a grip and realize that it's all good.

My dear sister shared a wonderful story from her own career that beautifully illustrates the point that it's not all about us. Here's how she learned this truth:

As Pharmacy Manager for a chain store, doing what I thought was a good job, I began to experience as much stress as a person can go through, but I knew in my heart that God would never give me more than I could handle. I was working 12-hour shifts, and there was so much work that I spent many days working more hours than that, only to have many things still left undone at the end of each day.

I was trusting God with all my heart when I was suddenly demoted from manager to staff pharmacist and was transferred to a new location that was many miles away from my home. I was devastated. After three decades of running my own business and then managing at this store, I could not believe this was happening. I thought this could not be God's plan for me since my former location was only five minutes from my home and I had loved that store.

But God's plans were indeed different. The new store I was placed in had equipment that was not familiar to me, the staff was much younger and could work rings around me, and I was made to feel like I was an outsider and unwanted. My husband and I prayed, and God let us know that this store was where I belonged, and He spoke to my heart, "Fear not for I am with thee, be not dismayed for I am thy God. I will strengthen thee. I will help thee" (Isaiah 41:10).

Day by day as I worked, it was unbearable in the pharmacy—my worst nightmare. The tension was great between the staff and myself, and every night when I would come home, I would tell my husband I wanted to leave, but he would remind me of what God had spoken to my heart and that I was placed in the store for God's purpose. What was His purpose? His purpose, as He continued to reveal to me, was to share the love of Jesus and to share His Word.

What transpired in those six years was absolutely amazing. It would take too much paper to go into the details of all the wonders that occurred during that time. From my being obedient to God to love others and to share His love with them, three staff members came to a saving knowledge of God for themselves and many others were comforted in many difficult situations. In looking back, it is easy to see the wisdom of God in having me there. He made everything work together for good, for His glory, and gave me a blessing as well. When I retired, I would have never expected all the tears and gifts that came from my customers and the staff. But most importantly, seeing those who once had no knowledge of God's love happily embracing it, was a blessing beyond compare.

As was evidenced by my sister's story, one of your purposes for being in your present job may be the most important: to share God's love with those you work with. As you continue your journey and aspire to achieve career success, let Principle 7 inspire you to stay focused on what really matters. Success isn't achieving what everyone has achieved or even achieving what everyone else thinks that you should achieve. Success is achieving everything you were designed by God to do—stepping into your purpose and pursuing it with integrity. Whatever He has planned for you (and that may include the career you are in right now), do it with enthusiasm, realizing that it is only part of the puzzle. Tomorrow, or next week, or even next year, you could be moved on to the next phase; but until then, you are where you are, and you want to be a good representative of all you have faith in. Stand firm, stay focused, and most of all, stop running. After all, God's purpose is all around you, and it's all good!

PART THREE

Survival Strategies for the Lion's Den

Wouldn't it be wonderful if everyone could go to work each day and have pleasant people to work with and challenges within easy reach? Arriving in your office, you would see smiling faces and people eager to help you, good people who turned into good friends, and no one screamed at you about a deadline or customer problem. All your co-workers would be eager to see you get ahead, and your boss mentioned your name for all the promotional opportunities. You would constantly receive pay increases and bonuses, and you went home at the end of the day completely stress free. Sounds like such a great place to work, doesn't it?

The problem is that the typical workplace doesn't resemble anything like what was just described. Although we are often fortunate enough to work in great office environments with great people, just as the garden of Eden had a serpent lying in wait for Eve so too in today's contemporary workplace, much too frequently, that same old serpent is just waiting for his next victim. Whether it takes the form of working with difficult people, having stress-filled assignments, being passed over for a promotion that we worked hard for, or getting fired, we have all spent some time in the proverbial lion's den. It's usually not a very comfortable place to be.

There are some time-honored strategies for surviving your time in the lion's den. And since you will probably find yourself there more than once, it's not a bad idea to develop some skills in this area. As people of faith, we know that the trials of our faith (lion's den experiences) teach us perseverance, and perseverance increases our character and produces hope. With that in mind, as uncomfortable as the lion's den may be, you can learn to embrace the fruit it will produce in your life if you allow God to refine your character and continue making you more like Him as you trust in Him.

No matter how long you spend in the lion's den, remember what was said of Daniel after he was taken out of it. Daniel 6:23 says, "Not a scratch was found on him because he had trusted in his God."

Chapter Thirteen

Difficult Bosses

Faith at Work Tip: Nothing is impossible with God and He will give you the grace you need to work with the leader He has placed in authority over you.

Servants, be submissive to your masters with all fear, not only to the good and gentle, but also to the harsh (1 Peter 2:18).

If you have managed to go through your entire career without working for at least one difficult person, you are truly one of the fortunate ones. In fact, one of the most common workplace complaints and one of the main reasons people leave their jobs in search of another is because of a difficult boss. You know the type. They're the ones who often put their careers ahead of everyone else's. They are the ones who give the impossible deadlines with no thought of the time it takes to actually get a project done. They are the ones who goof off all day long and then get down to seriously working a couple of hours before quitting time and expect you to work overtime just to help them finish a task that could have been finished earlier if they hadn't wasted so much time. They're the shouters and screamers, the work credit stealers, the politicians, and the people bashers. They come in all shapes and sizes, genders, and races. But they have one thing in common—we hate working for them.

Throughout his career, Daniel had some prize-winning difficult bosses. Remember King Nebuchadnezzar's impossible assignment? He had a dream that really disturbed him. He didn't know what the dream meant, but he knew that it was significant. He called in his staff who were trained in interpreting dreams but refused to tell them what the dream was. This was tough. Think about what you would do if your boss called you into her office and asked you to solve a problem but refused to tell you what the problem was. On top of that, imagine her telling you that if you didn't solve the problem, you would be fired on the spot. That is called being between a rock and a hard place.

After Daniel learned of this impossible request by his boss, he prayed to God that He would provide him with the wisdom and knowledge to not only know what the dream was but also to know what it meant. God mightily answered Daniel's prayer and gave him both the specifics and the meaning of the dream. Daniel shared this information with the king and ultimately everyone breathed easier. The problem was solved. They all lived happily ever after. It sounds like a fairy tale, doesn't it? But how does it really work today? We know how Daniel handled his difficult boss, but the question is how do you handle yours?

My friend Marjorie knew exactly how she was going to handle her difficult boss. Marjorie was a believer, but she couldn't stand Todd and thought he was a big phony. She had seen Todd behave in a mean-spirited way on many occasions, not only to her but also to many others on their team, and knew that he couldn't be trusted. So when she decided to resign from her position, she felt it was time to get even with Todd. In writing her resignation letter, she was sly. You see, she didn't attack Todd directly but instead wrote a wonderfully kind letter telling her superiors how honored she was to have worked for the company and how competent the other employees were. All of this was true, but she pointedly left Todd's name out of her letter. To make matters worse, knowing full well that he would be out of town, she slipped Todd's copy of the letter under his office door. She then overnight-expressed copies of her resignation to Todd's bosses in the corporate office, which she knew would be humiliating to Todd.

Admittedly, she felt pretty good about her actions until she took a Bible course and came across a scripture that said, "First go and be reconciled to your brother..." (Matt 5:24), which hit her squarely in the face. Boy, did she ever need to be reconciled! She got on her knees that night and asked God to forgive her and later called Todd and apologized to him for what she had done. Was this easy? Not at all, but she knew that in order to really worship God, she needed to be reconciled to the one who she felt had injured her at work. And she needed to seek his forgiveness for the actions she had taken to get even with him. She knew that God had forgiven her of so much, and she also needed to forgive Todd because of the mean-spirited way he had treated her.

We all have run into a few Todds and a few King Nebuchadnezzars in our lives, and some of us must confess that, unlike Daniel, we have responded just like Marjorie did initially because the temptation to get even is fierce. I know that in my own career one of the greatest challenges has been to work for someone whom I believed was difficult. Over time, as I reflect back on those instances, I have made a few observations. First, most people who truly are difficult to work with operate out of fear. Second, the difficulty of working together may exist because the style of working between the two people involved may be very different. Third, communicating honestly about situations as they occur really can be beneficial in improving a rocky working relationship.

In Daniel's day we can see these same observations at work. King Nebuchadnezzar was extremely frightened by the dream he had. He knew that it meant something important to his reign as king, but he didn't understand exactly what. That alone was very threatening to him, and a person who is afraid doesn't always think rationally, nor do they think about others. His style of working was autocratic. He gave orders and expected them to be carried out. He didn't accept excuses or explanations; he wanted results. He didn't believe in getting the team's suggestions or in having a democratic way of discussing a problem. Instead, he used his power to create fear in his team—intimidation to get the results that he wanted. And finally, he wasn't a good listener. That meant his relationships with his subordinates were greatly hampered because he simply wasn't a good communicator. The combination of these three could have resulted in disaster had it not been for the example that one man set by believing God was in control of the situation.

Is it possible for us to experience the same level of success when dealing with a difficult boss today as Daniel did? Having a difficult boss is the perfect time to dress for success. By operating in the truth—remembering that God is who He says He is and can do what He says He can do—we, too, can see that even the most difficult boss is not too hard for God, and therefore, someone whom we can learn to get along with.

Let me start with some examples from my own life. One of my first jobs after college was working for an oil company that drilled for oil primarily in the Middle East. Many of the managers of the company also came from the Middle East and had very different ideas about how women were to be treated in the workplace. My boss, in particular, expressed very little respect for women, and his actions did not contradict his beliefs. When I first began to work for him, many people warned me that he was very difficult to work for and encouraged me to keep one eye on my back. My boss did not disappoint his critics. He was obnoxious, rude, and condescending. But his worst character flaw was his inability to control his temper. When he became stressed out, he would often scream at everyone in the office. It was very demeaning to the team, and it really ticked me off. After all, I had grown up in an environment where grown men simply didn't express their displeasure through screaming, and this notion was completely foreign to me.

I remember once making an error in my work and he became so mad about it that he yelled at me in front of all my peers. I was mortified! I went into the restroom at work and burst into tears. I thought I had made a big mistake coming to work for this guy. But I was also determined to live my faith at work. I believed that God was strengthening my character and teaching me some important skills that I would need later in my career. After all, I knew that everyone wasn't always going to be a piece of cake to work with, so I wanted to learn how to deal with difficult people up front.

I began to ask God to help me better understand my boss. I prayed for him daily and tried very hard to excel at each assignment that he gave me. Before long, we began to talk about our lives outside of work, and I learned how hard it was for him to be so far away from his home and family. I also learned that he had a heavy weight resting on his shoulders because any failure at work was not only viewed in his culture as a failure to him but also to his entire family. As a result, he often operated under a fear of failure, and that affected how he treated others.

Before long, we became great friends. In fact, it reached a point that when he would start one of his screaming tirades, I would lift one eyebrow and look at him very sorrowfully, and inevitably, he would start laughing and apologize for having misbehaved. We worked together for almost two years, and my colleagues marveled at how well we got along. They often asked me how I was able to accomplish something that no one else had ever managed to do. I gave all the credit to God because I knew that He had answered my prayers to understand where my boss was coming from and to give me the ability to establish a better relationship with him.

On another occasion, I had to work for a person who I believed was difficult, but have since determined it wasn't that he was so difficult as much as it was that we just had a different style of working. Ben was a very precise kind of guy. In fact, he would have made a great accountant since he was sure to have all his i's dotted and his t's crossed. He didn't believe in having any fun at work. From the minute he hit the door, he was all work and no play. I can easily say that Ben thought that his main job was to make sure that the rest of us were working as hard as he was. Of course, none of us could outwork Ben, and frankly, most of us didn't want to. We were all young and fresh out of college and still saw work as just something you did when you finished college and certainly not as something to be taken too seriously. We didn't have the same mind-set that Ben had. At least I didn't.

My style of working was quite different from Ben's. I loved to talk with my colleagues and always wanted to think of ways to lighten things up a bit. If there was a birthday celebration, I was there. If someone wanted to stop by my desk and talk for a while, I dropped everything because I believed that people came first. I always believed in doing a great job, after all that was what I was paid to do. However, I was a firm believer (and still am) that the results were what counted and the method used to get to those results, as long as they were honest, weren't nearly as important. In other words, if someone could accomplish a task in one hour (that might have taken someone else two hours to complete) by being more efficient, I believed that person should have been rewarded (right?), and certainly not given more work.

Of course, that was the rub. Ben didn't think this way at all. If I completed a task really quickly, I wanted to be rewarded by having additional time to spend on break with my friends. However, Ben believed that he could heap more work on me, and that drove me nuts. In fact, everything about Ben drove me nuts. There was the way he hovered near my desk if anyone stopped by to talk with me, as though to say, "I'm watching you, and you need to get back to work." And there was the way he would inevitably appear in my work area if my phone rang, to make sure it wasn't a personal call. Even the way he was always on time for everything and never late to anything was annoying because it magnified my little imperfections. And of course, because he was never late, he absolutely didn't tolerate tardiness in anyone else. He didn't care if you had sick kids; he didn't care if your bus was late; he didn't care if there was an accident on the freeway; he believed that you should plan for every possibility. Ben's work style was to be perfect in every way, which in and of itself isn't a bad thing, but when taken to the extreme, it becomes legalistic. As a result, very few people enjoyed working with him, including me. Was I always right in my interactions with Ben? Heavens no! But it taught me a lot about the style of the people that I would ultimately work for. It also taught me the importance of appreciating their different styles as well as recognizing the need to accommodate those differences whenever possible. If there was one thing that I learned from Ben, it was that difficulties between people at work often result from the different styles and ways that they prefer to do their work. If you are laid back and have a tendency to move about your work day without a true sense of urgency and you work for someone who acts as if his hair is always on fire, you are probably going to find it difficult to work together. You may be an introvert, and your boss may be an extrovert. These differences can be something you either learn to appreciate or just tolerate.

I learned the importance of honest communication from Cindy. Cindy was leading a major project that I was a part of. The company that we worked for was going through a major reorganization that would result in systems changes, product changes, and people changes. My job was to define how this reorganization would affect the people processes, and as a team leader, I reported to Cindy. Cindy and I both had worked for the organization for several years, but she had worked in one part of the country, and I had been in another, so our paths had never crossed. At her staff meetings, she was prone to hog the agenda and usually liked listening to her own ideas best. She talked in sound bites, very fast, and frequently cut others off in mid-sentence. Her tendency was to be interested in any technical aspects of the project, but she didn't have the same level of interest in the people aspects of the project. Since that was the area I was responsible for, it seemed to me as though the work my team was responsible for didn't always get the same "air time" as the other teams.

Finally, one day after sensing again that my team's contribution was being discounted, I decided to invite her out for coffee. As we sat drinking our lattes, I shared my concerns with her. In the process, she agreed that she really didn't appreciate the work that my team did because it hadn't been her idea to have us join the project in the first place. One of her superiors had insisted that she add my team to the overall project, and as a result, she had reluctantly done so and had subconsciously decided that she would merely tolerate us and not really engage us in any meaningful way. Having her admit this was a breakthrough in our relationship, and before long, we agreed to start again with her giving my team a fair shot. Going forward, I knew that my team and I had something to prove to Cindy, and as always, I sought God's help in leading my team through the challenge. God didn't fail us, and over time, we were able to forge a solid relationship with Cindy and become recognized as a value-added part of the overall project team.

I share these stories not to toot my own horn, but to point out that in each instance the same power existed for me that existed for Daniel in his time, and it exists for everyone today. When faced with the challenge of working for a difficult boss, begin seeing it as an opportunity to express your faith at work. Start by focusing on three key questions that can help you troubleshoot the nature of your boss' difficult nature.

1. Is my boss operating from a spirit of fear?

The answer to this question may not be readily apparent because our bosses are in more powerful positions than we are at work; therefore, it is easy to begin thinking that they cannot possibly be afraid. But don't be deceived by appearances. Many times when people are most afraid, they bluster about attempting to look less vulnerable so that they can give the appearance that they are in control. This fear will look different in different people. For some, it may reveal itself through a constant need to put everyone else down. Through others, it may reveal itself through an impersonal style that discourages any type of personal intimacy. It can also reveal itself through behaviors that are threatening, rude, and condescending. However it reveals itself, be discerning to this spirit of fear and begin focusing on ways that you can help alleviate some of the stress that your boss may be feeling. Always remember that greater is He that is in you then he that is in the world.

2. Is my boss's work style different than mine?

A lot of difficulties can be eliminated if we first learn to understand how our bosses prefer to work. Do you have a boss who is disorganized and can't keep a calendar if her life depends on it, while you know chapter and verse what you plan to do with each minute of your day? Instead of seeing this as a difficulty, view it instead as an opportunity to help your boss by using one of your strengths to support her weakness. Or what if your boss is a stickler for details, and you tend to be more of a big-picture person? This can also be an opportunity for you to sharpen up your skills and become more detailed oriented. Regardless of the style differences, always realize that if you and your boss were exactly the same, one of you wouldn't be necessary. Begin seeing these differences as a means to grow in areas that you may need to develop.

3. Have I communicated honestly with my boss about these difficulties?

Sometimes, we have not because we ask not. Is it possible that you have never honestly communicated to your boss the impact that his or her behavior is having on you? You may be amazed to find that your boss is completely unaware of how he or she is perceived. In the same way, there may be aspects about working with you that are difficult, and you, too, may be unaware of your impact on others. When communicating honestly, be sensitive to timing and focus on using an "I" message. In other words, don't decide to have this conversation when your boss is in the middle of a work crisis. Instead choose a time when you know that the message might be more readily received. Don't use accusing language, which could possibly cause your boss to feel threatened, but instead use the "I" message. For example, if trying to communicate to your boss the impact her lack of organization is causing, instead of saying, "You are so disorganized; it's a miracle that you can get anything done around here." You may say something like this instead: "I think we would be much more productive if we became more organized in our work. I have some ideas on how we could do that." By using this approach, you have taken the sting out of your words. You have also created a collaborative environment that may improve your working relationship with your boss.

A final warning: Some bosses may never change. In those cases, continue to seek God's wisdom on what changes He wants to see in you through your circumstances and begin applying those lessons immediately. When God allows us to be in a tough spot, there is always a reason, and many times it is to teach us to trust in His sovereignty. Having a difficult boss is not easy, but through prayer and discipline, each of us can learn how to love those who seem unlovable and to submit to the authority that God has placed over us.

Chapter Fourteen

Co-Workers, Critics, and Competitors

Faith at Work Tip: Ask God to help you bless your colleagues and do good to them.

Bless those who persecute you; bless and do not curse (Romans 12:8).

Now let's discuss your co-workers. Have you ever worked around difficult people? Unless you are working on another planet, the answer to that question is probably, "yes." There is an old adage that says, "I would really love my job if it weren't for the people." How true that can be sometimes. The funny thing is that there are probably people out there saying the same thing about you, too. Many of our greatest challenges as well as opportunities for growth will come from our ability to get along well with others. In fact, it was probably one of the first measurements used to identify how well we were adapting to school. When I look at some of my old grammar school report cards, I see a notation that says, "Plays well with others." That simply meant that my social and interpersonal skills were developing appropriately.

Things haven't changed much since those grammar school days. Our ability to work well with other people can have an impact on everything else we do and how others perceive us. While working for an oil and gas company many years ago, in what was at the time my dream job, I was feeling pretty pleased with myself, thinking I was making all the right moves toward career greatness. After reading a book on dressing for success, I began wearing the "success suit" that the book suggested I purchase. Keep in mind that my job didn't require this, but since I was bent on getting ahead, I wanted to stand out in the crowd be noticeable to the higher ups, and outshine my peers. Along with that suit, came the attitude that I was better than everyone else, and I walked around that office as though I was God's gift to the working masses.

Right about that time, I begin to notice that a certain colleague, whom I will call Delma, didn't seem to like me. In fact, I believe that it would be a true statement that Delma hated my guts. I didn't let that bother me at first because I believed that Delma was just jealous of me, so it was her problem, not mine. Delma was fairly high in the corporate pecking order. She was the boss's secretary. This may not appear to be an important role to some, but I later learned that a boss's secretary can be the best friend you could ever have. Of course I didn't know that at the time. Instead, I treated Delma as though she were insignificant and certainly not as important as me. As a result, Delma started to flex her muscles. She made sure that the boss knew every mistake I made. On the occasions when I did try to sneak past her desk unnoticed, she always miraculously managed to be near my desk where she could observe my exact arrival time and of course report this to the boss as though she was the town crier.

At the time, I couldn't figure out what I had done to get on the wrong side of Delma. All I knew was that I got a knot in my stomach every time I had any interaction with her because I knew it was going to be unpleasant. So I thought I would sic God on Delma. I began to pray that He would really get her and show her who was boss. My prayers in those days went something like this:

> Lord, you know what a troublemaker Delma is for me. Why don't you deal with her Lord? I can't help that she's jealous of me Lord. I'm just trying to do my job and she thinks of every way possible to aggravate me. Lord, you've got to DO something about Delma.

I can't begin to tell you the number of prayers that went to heaven sounding just like that. I bombarded God with what He needed to do about Delma, giving specific instructions on how He could solve my dilemma. I couldn't wait for Him to take action.

Do you know that God never did deal with Delma? Instead, He began to work on me. He started to show me how I contributed to the problem I was experiencing with Delma. He pointed out my superior attitude, my laziness in not getting to work on time, and my short-sightedness in not extending a hand of friendship to Delma. God began to work on my character, and I thank Him that He did. I can't imagine what a pill I would be to work with today if God hadn't begun to straighten me out a long time ago. Am I perfect now? Absolutely not! However, I've learned some important lessons through experiences like that one and others that followed it that helped me learn to work better with those whom I encounter at work. These lessons have served me well as I realized that a lot of our ability to work well with others starts with us.

Playing Well With Others

Lesson 1—Stay Away from Office Gossip

Betsy really loved her job at a children's store that specialized in dolls. She had fun selling the products to her tiny customers. There was so much delight in their eyes when they came into the store to see their favorite doll and buy it for a special occasion. Betsy got along well with her co-workers, too. In fact, during the short time she had been there, she had made several friends. One in particular, Laura, had become a close friend, and they often spent time together outside of work.

One day, Laura asked Betsy if she would baby-sit her kids so that she and her husband could have a much-needed evening out. Betsy gladly agreed and spent the next Friday night at Laura's house watching her children. When Laura and her husband came home that evening, it was obvious to Betsy that they had had a little bit too much to drink and were clearly enjoying themselves. She wished them a good evening and went home. However, the next day at work Betsy told her other co-workers all about Laura and her husband having come home a little tipsy. The story amused her co-workers, and Betsy didn't think anything more about it. Imagine her surprise when she began to notice that Laura was no longer speaking to her. At first, she thought Laura was simply in a bad mood. Whenever she approached Laura, the woman acted as though she didn't want to talk, and when she did talk, her answers were short and curt.

Two weeks passed, and the environment at the store was noticeably icy. Finally, Betsy decided to ask Laura what was wrong. Laura blurted out, "I really didn't appreciate you talking behind my back. I thought you were my friend." What ensued can only be described as the beginning of warfare. Betsy, of course, denied having said anything that was harmful about Laura. Laura didn't believe her and began to carry a grudge. Each of them tried to get the other co-workers to take sides and neither of them ever spoke to the other again.

What happened here? It is a story that is played out every day in workplaces everywhere: co-workers gossiping about one another. Some of it may be intentional and some may be unintentional, but it is always harmful. Would it surprise you to know that Betsy was a Christian and a person of deep faith in God? It shouldn't. As the saying goes, Christians aren't perfect, they're simply redeemed. The true lesson here is to avoid being in situations that lend themselves to gossip and intrigue. If you stay in the workplace for any amount of time, this issue will challenge you. Gossip is more popular at work than are sports, and everyone does it. It's grown to an epidemic proportion. Those that don't gossip are truly unique and viewed as peculiar. However, staying out of the middle of gossip is one of the best things we can do for others and ourselves. If you truly want to get along with your colleagues, don't say anything about them to others that you would have to defend if faced by them about it.

Lesson 2—Be Careful of the Dog that Always Brings the Bone

Minnie was a sweet kind person who was loved by everyone who worked with her. She always had an encouraging word to say to her colleagues and could always be found helping others. Most people confided in Minnie because they knew that anything told to her would stay "in the vault." Minnie's only character flaw (if it could be called that) was her trusting nature. She had a tendency to take people at face value without using her discernment to discover their true intentions.

One of her co-workers, Lucy, came to her one day and shared with her some of the problems she was experiencing with another employee named Jean. It was not unusual for Lucy to come to Minnie about work complaints. She had a tendency to be a bit of a tattletale and a whiner.

So Minnie heard her grievances as she had done many times before. Minnie was aware that Jean had had problems with other staff members as well and generally wasn't trusted by most. As Minnie listened to Lucy's complaints, she agreed with most of what Lucy was saying because she had heard similar complaints from others. She didn't share any of this with Lucy, but rather, listened sympathetically. Finally, Lucy confessed that she didn't trust Jean. Minnie believed it would encourage Lucy to know that she was probably wise not to trust Jean, so she told her that and went on about her work.

Later that day, Lucy returned to tell her that Jean had made an interesting comment about Minnie. Jean had said that Minnie wasn't to be trusted either. Upon hearing this, Minnie became very upset because she realized that Lucy had shared her earlier comments with Jean. She was devastated. She had tried to be helpful only to have her words used against her.

Minnie learned a difficult lesson that day—be careful of the dog who always brings you the bone, or in other words, the person who is always talking to you about others is more than likely talking to others about you. This type of person is commonly seen in the workplace. They are the ones who keep things stirred up. They instigate issues between colleagues. They are constantly looking for "the dirt" on others and love to pass it around creating disharmony in the workplace. They are quick to give relational advice and eager to hear what is being said about other people in the office. Beware of these types. Their approach is always friendly at first, but their intentions and their actions are lethal. When dealing with co-workers like these, be wise as a serpent but gentle as a dove.

Lesson 3—Rise Above Office Politics

If you think about it, the story of Daniel in the lion's den is a perfect example of office politics. In Daniel 6 he was minding his own business at work and doing a great job of it. He had received promotion after promotion and was due to be made the department manager. His co-workers got really jealous of his success and couldn't stand the thought of him being their boss. So they came up with a plan to bring Daniel down a notch or two.

They knew that Daniel was a very religious fellow and that he prayed everyday, so they proposed a new work rule to the king. They suggested that no one be allowed to petition any god or man other than the king. Anyone caught praying to a god would be promptly thrown into the lion's den for their supper. The king thought highly of Daniel and had no way of knowing that this was a plot to destroy him. Instead, being of the kingly sort, he believed that his subjects were merely suggesting this rule to please and honor him. He signed it into policy only to learn later that Daniel was in violation of the new rule. He was greatly distressed because he knew that he had no choice but to have Daniel thrown into the den of lions since a king could not undo his own edicts. And so, Daniel was thrown into the lion's den, with not much hope of surviving.

Isn't that exactly how office politics work in the twenty-first century? People are constantly examining their success by someone else's success and trying to figure out how to be better than the other guy. One-upmanship and attempts to impress the boss are constantly going on. Power plays, cutting throats, back stabbing: These are common actions in the high stakes game of office politics. They are unavoidable; therefore, how you deal with them becomes critically important. As with any other type of adversity, people of faith must resolve to rise above the fray. We are not promised a life that is free from adversity. We are promised that God will be with us in the middle of any adversity and will show us the right path to take, just as He did with Daniel.

So what is the best way to deal with office politics? First, be aware that they exist. Realize that some of the best political players would not describe themselves as political. They will always refer to others as being political, but never refer to themselves in that way. They're simply trying to get their job done. Don't be deceived. Some of the best office politicians are typically those who are very good at exploiting those who are less skillful at the game than they are. They are good students of human behavior and quickly figure out each person's hot buttons. They are especially knowledgeable about the hot buttons of those in power and authority. Think about Daniel's co-workers; they knew exactly what would please the king and how to use the king's ego to attempt to bring harm to Daniel. And the same is true today. We are surrounded by people who are looking for any chink in our armor, which is why we are encouraged to put on the whole armor of God to withstand the fiery arrows that will be coming our way.

What is that armor? It is truth, righteousness, peace, faith, salvation, and the Word of God. By always speaking the truth, doing what is right, seeking peace rather than discord, believing in faith that God is there to fight our battles, accepting His salvation and plan for our lives, and believing what God's Word says about us, we can withstand and rise above any political attack.

Abigail saw the power of wearing God's whole armor in a very political situation at her job. She had prayed for an opportunity to relocate after having graduated from a very prestigious African-American university. She was excited about pursuing a career in her major and landed a job with a large technology company. After completing one year in her position with them, she became a marketing support specialist within the company. After extensive training and four months on the new job, she was laid off. This was a huge disappointment for someone so anxious to utilize her business skills and gain some experience.

Despite her situation, she continued to trust God that she would find another opportunity, and while looking, she did volunteer work at her church, helping others. It was during this time that she happened to have a telephone conversation with one of her former teammates and was told by her teammate that she had recently changed her ethnic status to minority. Her teammate had been encouraged to do this so that she could remain employed with the company during the staff reductions. Abigail realized that while politics had been used in a way that negatively affected her continued employment with the company, she still believed that God had a plan for her.

One week later, she received a call from the same company and was offered a job in another location for the same position she had previously. Abigail insists that it was her faith that helped her during this time. She could have given into the fear of not knowing her future or how she would earn a living. Or she could have allowed the bitterness of office politics to consume her. Instead, it was her faith that strengthened her resolve to be steadfast in her walk of faith and to believe that God was still God and was always there to help her during a time of adversity. Sometimes, we have no control over the political situations that we find ourselves in. We do, however, have control over how we respond to our situations, and Abigail passed that test with flying colors.

Lesson 4—Be Willing to Serve

This is a tough one. Being a servant has such negative connotations in our society. We typically think of servants as being powerless, weak, submissive, and under someone else's control. Of course, since most of us are constantly trying to control everything in our lives, being a servant, especially to those we work with, isn't that appealing. And yet, it is exactly what we are encouraged to do as people of faith.

When Jesus walked on the earth, He was constantly seeking ways to serve others. There are many examples of how He served. Think about it—He washed His disciples feet. Try to get a picture of doing something like that to some of the people whom you work with. I wouldn't recommend that you start snatching their socks off just yet, but there is a clear principle here that can help make the work environment a better place to be. The principle is this: It's not all about YOU! In fact, you were created to serve—first to serve God, then to serve your family and others. By understanding what you were created to do, you begin to have a distinct advantage over those working alongside you because you will be walking in your purpose.

This idea of serving others is not a new one. Just ask my friend Carol. Carol is a professional organizer and has her own business designed to serve and help others become organized. She really thought she had a servant's heart. Because she believed this about herself, she sent out a promotional piece several months ago to get some work. She advertised that she would do free consultations in the hope that it would lead to long-term assignments. She believed herself to be a gracious-hearted person who wanted to share her talent for organization with those less organized.

A woman who needed help from Carol called her, and Carol went to give her a free consultation. This woman was moving to a bigger home and had already started packing. Carol was delighted to help her, and they hit it off immediately. Carol was thinking about all the money she would make from this woman hiring her for the project. She spent over two hours providing her with many wonderful ideas on how to organize her new home. Afterwards, the woman called her and said she wasn't going to need Carol after all.

Carol was so angry that she couldn't see straight. She became convinced that the woman never had any intention of hiring her but simply wanted the free consultation. Unfortunately, Carol let her anger show in her voice, and the woman hung up knowing that Carol was not in the least bit pleased. As Carol looked back on the experience, she had to acknowledge that although she intended to serve by giving of herself freely with no expectations, her actions painted another picture altogether. Carol admits now that she missed an opportunity to demonstrate God's unselfish love and a servant's heart.

Carol's response was a natural one that I'm sure we can all relate to. But it doesn't change the fact that we are seeking ways to work well together with others. When we serve others in our work, even when they don't deserve it, we are replicating the very behavior that God exhibits in our lives everyday. After all, our source is not our clients, or our employer, or our co-workers. The source for everything we need is God. He is the one who provides the opportunities to earn a living, to gain wealth, and to succeed at our work. It all comes from Him, and once we understand that, we begin to see our acts of service to others as a way to serve Him. So freely serve the ones you work with, being assured that whether or not they appreciate it, the One who is most important already does.

Chapter Fifteen

Impossible Work Assignments

Faith at Work Tip: Even when things seem chaotic, God is still in control

We are hard-pressed on every side, yet not crushed; we are per-plexed, but not in despair, persecuted, but not forsaken; struck down, but not destroyed (2 Corinthians 4:8-9).

One of the biggest challenges for us as believers within the work-place is to believe that God is in control of all circumstances that come our way. In our hearts, we know that a righteous person's steps are or-dered by the Lord, but in practice it is sometimes difficult to keep that thought in our heads as we face difficulties in the workplace.

Julia learned this lesson as her company went through a rather sizeable merger. Her company had employed Julia for over a decade when she heard the announcement that the company had been bought by a competitor. Being a person of faith, Julia didn't really feel worried about the merger because she knew that God was her source and all her employment opportunities were in His hands. She had an important position in the company. She was the head of the operations depart-ment and had experienced success while performing that role. But she was a realist and, therefore, was not optimistic about her chances of re-maining in the same position. After all, the other company already had an operations manager, and it wasn't going to be necessary to keep them both.

As the months passed, Julia waited to hear the outcome of the se-lection process. The senior manager of the division had interviewed her, and he seemed interested in finding a role for her. She was actually feeling pretty happy as she thought of all the possibilities and opportunities that might surface as a result of the merger. She was fully expecting that God would amaze her by having this new management team identify some brilliant new role designed especially for her. Soon, she was called into a meeting and told that she had not received the top job of operations manager. As she had expected, that position would go to the person who was already doing the job for the acquiring firm. But she was offered another job in which she would report to the operations manager. It was a job that she had done several years before in her career, and it clearly didn't have the size or scope of responsibility that she had become accustomed to. She was shocked! She thought there must be some mistake. Couldn't they see all her talent would be wasted in this new job? She told them that she needed to think about the offer. Leaving the meeting a little shaken, she went immediately in search of God.

Her conversation with God a little while later went a bit like this:

God did you hear about this ridiculous job they offered me? I could do that job in my sleep. This can't be Your plan for me. After all, You have a good plan for my life, and this is not a good plan. Lord, if I turn down this job, I won't receive my severance benefits because they have said that this job is an equivalent job to my old one. Now, Lord, you know that is the biggest lie ever told because there is no way that this job is the same in scope as my old job. Clearly, they want to make it seem so, to avoid paying the severance. What on earth am I going to do? God, I don't want this job. I want to be doing something meaningful, with purpose, and that is challenging. You know my heart, Lord, and this is simply not the *job for me.*

For days, Julia debated with God about this job. In her mind, this was an impossible assignment. Her pride was hurt that she would even be asked to do a job so obviously beneath her capabilities. She still found it difficult to believe that God would really intend for her to do it, and yet deep in her spirit, she could sense His presence and His gentle voice saying, "My ways are not your ways, and my thoughts are higher than your thoughts." But she argue with Him and told Him of the kinds of work she should be involved in and how she would be so bored if she took this job. Yet, no matter how much she debated, she did not regain her peace until she finally resolved in her heart to accept the job that had been offered to her. Of course, things didn't become easier simply because she acquiesced. Instead, it was a daily challenge for her to remain humble and do her job despite having feelings that she had in some way been wronged.

Julia's experience is not uncommon to many believers. In fact, as each of us go on our spiritual journeys, we face the daily temptation to doubt that God is in control of all our circumstances. It is easy to believe that He is in control when things are going great at work: We are getting promoted, we receive a long expected raise, we are acknowledged with a special reward for a job well done or we get hired for that "dream" job. On the other hand, it's not so easy to see Him at the reins when something is amiss. In many ways, if we were to admit it, we think God is just as surprised as we are when things don't turn out as we expected them to. What do we do when we have been handed an assignment that we perceive to be impossible?

There really are two choices. We can decide to take the "Jonah" route, or we can take the victorious route. But let's first explore the Jonah route.

Jonah was one of the original evangelists. His work involved preaching and telling people about the good news of God's grace. But there was a group of people that he simply couldn't stand. Frankly, he hoped that they would never learn of God's grace because he ultimately hoped that they would get what was coming to them. This nation of people had been enemies of his nation for many years, and there had been animosity between the countrymen for as long as anyone could remember. As a result, Jonah never gave any thought to evangelizing these people; he thought they were worthless and didn't deserve God's grace.

But one day, Jonah received a divine assignment. God spoke to Jonah directly and told him to go to this group of people and tell them how they could receive mercy for their wrongdoing. Jonah couldn't believe it—God couldn't really be serious! Jonah decided immediately that he was not going to take the assignment, but that he would instead pursue another job opportunity as far away from God's assignment as possible. Jonah didn't realize it at the time, but he had just made the biggest mistake of his career.

As a result of his refusal to accept his divine assignment, Jonah ended up in the ocean after being tossed off the very ship that was to carry him to the assignment he had chosen for himself. And to make matters worse, a huge fish came along and swallowed him up, and he remained inside the fish for three days. After he came to his senses and humbly accepted the job God had for him, he was released from the fish and was able to go on to meet his destiny.

The Jonah route clearly has its disadvantages. Any time we, as people of faith, forget who is really calling the shots in our lives, we set in motion circumstances that are ultimately not going to be to our liking. Even the most difficult job assignment has to be viewed through the lenses of God's sovereignty. The assignment that you may be given today, while impossible to you, is no surprise to God and, therefore, not outside His control. In fact, it is through some of the most difficult assignments that we are given that we learn the most about God's character and what He is capable of doing in a yielded life.

Having explored the Jonah route, what is the alternative? To demonstrate this, we must return once again to our guide, Daniel. Midway through Daniel's career, he had yet another new boss. King Nebuchadnezzar had died and Belteshazzar was on the throne. It is typical in everyone's career that when a new boss comes on the scene, it's like starting over. They don't know you, and you don't know them, so no matter how many great things you might have done in the past, you start proving your capabilities again, to the new boss.

That is exactly the position that Daniel found himself in. After having achieved great career success under Nebuchadnezzar's leadership, with Belteshazzar as king, Daniel was once again an unknown entity. In fact, Belteshazzar threw a big party for many of his top officials, and Daniel wasn't even invited. However, during the party, something strange occurred. Some writing appeared on the wall of the party room in a language that no one could interpret. The king and his guests had been drinking quite a bit, so it would be understandable if they had thought they were hallucinating. But that wasn't the case, and Belteshazzar became very afraid, especially when some of his top advisors could not tell him what the writing meant.

It just so happened that the queen had heard about Daniel and suggested that Belteshazzar send for him because she understood him to
be a person of great skill, insight, and wisdom. When Daniel arrived at
the party and surveyed the scene, he knew immediately what the
writing said and was able to provide the interpretation. That was the
hard part because the writing basically said that Belteshazzar's
kingdom was finished. Now anyone who has ever been a student of
biblical writing knows that the last thing you want to tell a king is that
his days are numbered. Imagine if you were in Daniel's shoes and you
had to walk into your boss' office and tell her something that you knew
may make her furious enough to take it out on you and possibly even
fire you. That was the assignment that Daniel was basically given to do.

So how did he handle this tough assignment? In the same manner
that we have come to see him handle most of his career assignments.
He didn't blink an eye but told with great compassion the truth about
the king's future. Was this easy to do? Probably not. But was it the right
thing to do? Absolutely! Daniel had long since learned that his job was
not merely a way to earn a living. He understood that he had been
placed there for a purpose and that he needed to be mindful of the purpose everyday. He experienced victory after victory in both good times
and bad because he had a keen understanding of that truth.

So, how do we take the route to victory instead of taking the Jonah
route? And how do we continue to live by faith at work when we haven't
quite convinced ourselves that God has everything under control?

First, we must acknowledge the truth and confess it to God. One of
the best things about the Psalms is the transparency that existed in
David's relationship with God. When you read the Psalms, you see that
at some points he was exhilarated and at other points he was in the
depths of despair, but that at all times he had an honesty and truthful-
ness that we all can learn from. By modeling David's honesty with God,
we too can begin to share honestly our doubts and fears about our circumstances. Many times, just confessing that we have doubts opens the
door for God to take us to a new level of intimacy with Him. His primary goal is to create a change in who we are rather than to always
change our circumstances to fit what we think they ought to be.

By telling God about our doubts and fears in the middle of our circumstances, we can also begin to ask for help to overcome that which

has us most fearful. In fact, we should ask ourselves what we are most afraid of. When we identify what has us "gasping for breath," we can lay that issue before God and wait for Him to correct our thinking about the matter. In prayer, and by meditating on God's Word, we will find that our thinking becomes less finite and will ultimately change to cause us to see the infinite possibilities with God.

As we face what we think are impossible tasks, we can begin to focus on the practical solutions that may help us to accomplish our overall goals. In other words, are there resources that we need that could help us? Are there certain skills that we ourselves may not possess but that may exist in some of our co-workers? Is it possible that we need to negotiate more time to complete an assignment or need to ask for the assistance of others? Or is it possible that the assignment isn't impossible, but the problem is simply that we just don't want to do it?

Thinking about practical solutions can help ignite ideas in our minds that give God something to work with as we put ourselves confidently in His hands. As we begin this process, some of our biggest fears will diminish as we begin to think about the possibilities instead of the impossibilities.

That's what Julia did. She realized that her biggest fear was that she would be considered insignificant. She saw her new job as an insignificant one in the whole scheme of things, and although she was being paid the same and her benefits weren't changing, she still believed that she, too, had become insignificant. However, once she humbly submitted to the authority of God, she realized that His goal for her was to continue to share His love with others in spite of what she perceived to be the wrong that had been done to her. She began to do her job with enthusiasm, even when she didn't feel enthusiastic. She never conveyed to her team or her boss that she was not 100 percent on board and went out of her way to help others while in her new role. Anyone watching Julia would have believed she had been promoted rather than the opposite. And on those days when she was tempted to get down in the dumps about her circumstances, she continued to seek God's counsel, and He continued to lead her day by day, step by step. After a while, she realized that the assignment hadn't been so impossible after all. The truth was that her attitude had been the troublemaker and her focus had been on her will, rather than God's will, for her life. Once she realized that, she became more open to the changes God wanted to make in her and began to see her assignment through His eyes.

It is important to remember that it is not the destination of our spiritual lives that is so important because, after all, if you are a follower of Christ, then your destination is already secure. It is, however, always the journey that counts. God wants us to know Him. He wants us to know His nature and to believe that He will do everything He promised. This seldom means that things will always go our way. But it does mean that as we live the life of faith, we will come to know Him and trust that He is who He says He is—the creator of the universe and our heavenly Father; therefore, He truly is in control.

Chapter Sixteen

The Success Idol

Faith at Work Tip: Seek God's definition of success and pursue it wholeheartedly

Let nothing be done through selfish ambition or conceit, but in lowliness of mind let each esteem others better than himself (Philippians 2:3).

Catherine was a woman who had worked most of her adult life. In fact, she couldn't remember a time when she hadn't worked. Her goal was to become a success by making so much money that she would at some point be able to tell her boss and everyone else at work to "shove it" and quit. This one goal became the most important thing in her life. She wanted to be successful, and her measuring stick was to make money and plenty of it. To her, a sign of true success was to be a millionaire by the time she was 35. As a result, she did whatever was necessary to make money. If it meant telling a small lie to get an account, she would do it. If it meant cutting corners in her work, she would do that too. Her philosophy was that the end justifies the means. After all, didn't God want her to prosper as He had said in the third book of John? She planned to end up with lots of money no matter what means it took to get it.

Interestingly enough, Catherine would have described herself as a person of faith. She went to church faithfully every Sunday, and she professed to love God and believed that He did, in fact, exist. It was very common to see Catherine reading her Bible at work each day. Usually, she would arrive early so that she could have a cup of coffee and still have time to read the Bible before the start of her workday. Catherine's colleagues had learned not to approach her when she was reading her Bible. They had learned from experience that she became very irritated when she was interrupted and would say very sarcastically to the intruder, "Can't you see I'm reading my Bible?" Catherine's nasty attitude when reading her Bible had become a joke among her co-workers. They would frequently tell new employees, "Don't mess with Catherine when she's reading that Bible or she will bite your head off." It became clear to everyone that whatever Catherine was reading in that Bible, it certainly wasn't improving her attitude.

You may also be wondering how Catherine could faithfully read her Bible everyday and yet have the beliefs about money that she did and behave as she did to her co-workers. Certainly Catherine's true commitment to God was questionable. What was more obvious was Catherine's commitment to achieving success. Catherine had allowed attaining success to become an idol in her life. She worshiped it and would do anything for it. Despite her expressed love for God by reading her Bible and going to regular church services, she loved making money more. She was trusting in her ability to make herself successful rather than trusting in God.

While at work, there are many things that tempt us to trust in something else rather than to trust in a God who loves us and cares about us. In fact, many of these things may become idols in our lives. What exactly is an idol? Webster defines "idol" as "a representation or symbol of an object of worship; a false god; a form or appearance visible but without substance; an object of extreme devotion." Although God does indeed want us to live prosperous and successful lives, we must first learn to define success the way He does and not allow the mere idea of success to become an idol. If we define success by the amount of money we earn, the position we hold, or the power and authority we have at work, we will miss the deeper meaning of success as only God can teach us. Before we know it, our trust in God will lessen, while our trust in ourselves and our capabilities will grow. Being able to remain balanced in our spiritual journey while achieving success at work is a matter of survival to the believer.

Daniel's friends, Shadrach, Meshach, and Abednego, had achieved significant success during their careers while working for the king.

However, there came a time when their faith was put to the test. Were they beginning to trust in their own capabilities, or did they hold success lightly in order not to compromise their deeper faith in God? Here is how Daniel tells the story:

King Nebuchadnezzar made a golden statue 90 feet tall and nine feet wide and set it up on the plain of Dura in the province of Babylon. Then he sent messages to the princes, prefects, governors, advisers, counselors, judges, magistrates, and all the provincial officials to come to its dedication. When all these officials had arrived and were standing before the image, a herald shouted out, "People of all races and nations and languages, listen to the king's command! When you hear the sound of the horn, flute, zither, lyre, harp, pipes and other instruments, bow to the ground to worship King Nebuchadnezzar's golden statue. Anyone who refuses to obey will immediately be thrown into a blazing furnace."

So at the sound of the musical instruments, all the people, whatever their race or nation or language; bowed to the ground and worshiped the statue. But some of the astrologers went to the king and informed on the Jews. They said to King Nebuchadnezzar, "Long live the king! You issued a decree requiring all the people to bow down and worship the gold statue when they hear the sound of the musical instruments. That decree also states that those who refuse to obey must be thrown into a blazing furnace. But there are some Jews—Shadrach, Meshach, and Abednego—who you have put in charge of the province of Babylon. They have defied Your Majesty by refusing to serve your gods or to worship the gold statue you have set up" (Daniel 3:1-12).

The following are the circumstances of the dilemma that Shadrach, Meshach, and Abednego found themselves in:

1. They were advisers to the king.
2. The king had established an idol for all the people and government officials to worship, thereby, showing their loyalty to him.
3. They were forbidden to worship any type of idol because of God's commandments.
4. To disobey the king would mean physical death.
5. To disobey God would mean spiritual death.

What should they do? Disobey the king or disobey God? This is the question that taunts many of us each day as we work diligently at our jobs. The idol that Daniel's friends faced may appear different to the contemporary believer, but the dilemma is always the same. These guys were human. It would be natural for them to want to retain the good relationship that they had with their boss, the king.

What was this idol really? What are some of the idols that the twenty-first century person of faith confronts in the workplace? There are many, but the one that seems to be the most attractive is the drive to succeed. The search for success can take on many different forms. It can be striving for position and power, money, rewards, or promotions. Whatever it may be, the desire to succeed is not in and of itself a bad thing. It is only when our drive to succeed replaces God in our lives that the dilemma is set in motion. When confronted with this, the person of faith is challenged to either trust God, or to bow down and worship.

Do we do whatever is necessary to maintain the level of success that we have achieved, including compromising our principles? Or do we recognize that there is no true success if God is not in the mix? A common mistake that many people of faith make is forgetting what should be their true motivation for working.

Success Imitators

Our reason for working should always be one that is motivated by our love for God; instead, we can become deluded into working for our ill-defined idea of success and therefore confuse the real thing with cheap imitations. We see this in every aspect of life. Instead of butter, we use margarine. Pseudo-antiques are being passed off as real antiques, and generic brands replace designer labels. The same is true at work. Your desire may be to set a great example in the office and to show your co-workers that, as a person of faith, you stand for excellence and hard work. While this is a great motivation, don't fall into the trap of believing that God measures your performance with the same yardstick that the world does. In fact, in the workplace, some worldly definitions of success have come to be accepted by many people as common wisdom.

We must be able to identify some of the "success imitators" that can sometimes beset the unsuspecting person of faith. I am speaking of those cheap imitations that are not inherently bad, but that shouldn't be confused with the real thing. These imitations, when achieved, give us a false sense of accomplishment at first, but later leave us feeling empty and without purpose if they are our sole means of measuring our success. The easiest to identify and the strongest imitators of success are money, position, and power. There are very few who can withstand the lure of these three and fewer still who can handle having them without becoming conceited and prideful. Even the most diligent person of faith must constantly check her heart to be sure that having gained any one of these three, she remains focused on God's definition of success.

Clearly, it is acceptable for one of our motivations for working to be to earn a living. In fact the Bible specifically says, "Those who work deserve their pay" (1Timothy 5:18). It is natural to desire enough financial earnings from a job to provide for the needs of our families and to live without worry of being able to meet financial commitments. However, the Bible also warns us that, "...the love of money is at the root of all kinds of evil. And some people, craving money, have wandered from the faith and pierced themselves with many sorrows" (I Timothy 6:10). When it is money that we love, we mistakenly believe that it can solve all our problems. When it is God that we love, we see Him as our sole provider and everything we have (our jobs and our money) as being a direct result of His provision.

The difference in working to earn a living and working because we love money is evident by how we view God as a provider. Are you measuring your success in life based on how much money you are earning? Do you spend a considerable amount of time contemplating how you can get more? Do you see your job as your key source of gaining money? By really thinking about how you would answer any of these questions, you may begin to gain some insight into how you view money as it relates to your professional success. Keep in mind that it is common and tempting to measure your success in this manner because it is a key measuring stick in the workplace and in society in general. But it remains a success imitator.

What about power? How does it imitate success? Belinda would know. She had gained plenty of it in her career. She had graduated first in her class and was recruited by some of the top firms in her industry. After agreeing to join one of them, it didn't take long for her to advance up the career ladder, and within a relatively short time, she was running a large division with hundreds of employees. The rise to the top was exhilarating, especially when she realized how much power came with it. Belinda loved the way subordinates treated her so deferentially, and it pleased her when with just a mere shift of her eyebrow at a meeting, others were made to swallow uncomfortably, wondering what she was thinking or how it would effect them. The more power that she gained, the more isolated she became because, in truth, people were afraid of Belinda. She had a reputation for using her power for her own professional gain. She always managed well, but for those who worked around her and below her, she was someone to watch out for.

Belinda would have described herself as a very successful person. She had gained power, but at the end of her career, she was a very lonely woman. She didn't understand how someone who had achieved as much professional clout as she had could find herself with such an empty life. She had placed establishing her career above establishing any long-term personal relationships, and as a result, did not have a family or any close personal friends. Later in her career, as her professional power started to diminish, she found that her business associates were merely that, and eventually there were fewer and fewer of them that she could really count on. She had idolized her success to that point that it was the driving motivator in her professional career. Ultimately, she had defined her success by power and had found it to be a cheap imitation of true success.

So What's Wrong With Wanting To Succeed?

You may be asking, "What's wrong with wanting to succeed?" Nothing. In fact, if we do our jobs with excellence and treat our colleagues with respect, it is likely that it will lead to a position higher up the corporate ladder, and success may follow. The issue is not one of having the desire to succeed by achieving a better position. The issue is that of having the desire to succeed at any cost and using the wrong compass to determine what true success is all about. Remember, our reason for being in the workplace is not only about us. If God has given us the ability to work, then He has placed us in our jobs to be a beacon of His love to others. With this in mind, our focus turns away from success as we define it and turns to success as God defines it. Sometimes, we incorrectly define our success based on the level of our job title and the authority it gives us in the company. But God's definition of success is that we bloom wherever He has planted us. We are not to determine our success by what other people are doing; we are to determine our success by whether we are doing what God has assigned us to do and doing it well.

So, how do you determine if your drive to succeed has become your work idol? Consider the following:

1.   What is motivating you to work? Is it merely to get ahead or are you motivated by your love for God and your desire to be used by Him?

2.   How would you feel if you were not selected for the promotion you have been dreaming of? Would you be naturally disappointed but at peace because you know that God has something better? Or would you be really envious of the person who got the promotion and secretly wishing they would fail?

3.   Do you do your job enthusiastically even when the boss is not around, as though working for the Lord? Or do you work hard only when you are certain of its being noticed by your boss and others who you believe can help you succeed?

If we are really honest with ourselves in considering these questions, it becomes easy to see whether we are living our faith at work or simply doing time in pursuit of the success idol.

If that is the case, we can return to God and ask him to help us desire success the way He defines it and obtain those promotions that really count in His book. What can we do to be promoted by God? We can start specializing in those principles that result in eternal rewards, better known as the Promotion Principles:

P—Place God's agenda at the top of your "to do" list. Ask him before starting your work day, "What are your priorities for me today God?" And then trust him to respond as he did to Isaiah, "I will be gracious if you ask for help. I will respond instantly to the sound of your cries" (Isaiah 30:19).

R—Read God's Word daily. It is only by knowing the Word of God that you can truly understand his character and begin to emulate his behavior.

O—Offer yourself to others as one who is willing to serve just as though you are serving the Lord (Col. 3:23).

M—Meet with the Lord daily. Schedule an appointment with Him and use that time to meditate on God's words.

O—Obey God and do what He tells you to do in your time alone with Him.

T—Thank God for the blessing of your job, even on those days when it may not feel like a blessing.

I—Imitate the love God has for you by sharing His love with those you work with.

O—Observe the situations that God allows in your life and be alert to opportunities to share the message of Christ.

N—Nullify all real or imagined injustices done to you by others by having a forgiving heart.

It is only by putting these principles into practice each day that we begin to receive God's promotions in our lives. When we seek God first and make His priorities our priorities, He promises that all these other things will be given to us. What was He referring to when He said, "other things"? It is those things which are important and necessary to fulfill His purpose in our lives. One of His purposes for us is that we succeed at the work He has given us to do. Learn to define success in a new way, and you will be amazed at the difference it will make in your life.

My friend Andrew did exactly that. Andrew had been working for many years as a banking professional. He had started his career as a teller in a financial services company but gradually, through hard work and determination, had moved into a position of responsibility in the finance department. Andrew loved his job and did it well. It wasn't long before Andrew was lured away from that company to work for another firm, which offered him an even higher position making more money than he had ever earned before. Year after year, Andrew enjoyed the rewards of his hard work. He was loved by his colleagues and his superiors. In fact, it wasn't long before Andrew became a senior officer in his firm and had national responsibility for a large department. It would have been easy for Andrew to forget who his true source of success was and to begin to attribute his success to himself. But one day, things begin to change for Andrew.

It all started when he got a new boss. This boss was considered brilliant by many in the industry. He definitely exhibited the intelligence to warrant his reputation; however, he was also considered tough and insensitive by many. It wasn't unusual for him to publicly humiliate subordinates or to use profane language that was directed at them. It wasn't long before Andrew's boss began to recruit other leaders who were exactly like he was. All of them were focused on one thing: to win no matter what the cost. They interpreted winning to mean succeeding and becoming the most powerful people in the industry. This was all very distressing to Andrew because it appeared as though, no matter what he did, he could not please his new boss and, therefore, he did not fit in with his new team. Andrew describes the encounters this way:

Many times it was only God's Word that gave me the strength to get through a day, a meeting, or other situations when I felt personally attacked or found myself and others being criticized and embarrassed in the presence of others. There were many days in which my boss behaved in ways that were an affront to my Christian values. I prayed before and during these meetings with him for the Lord to give me the strength to not act the same way in anger and frustration, to be calm, and to not compromise my own integrity.

When your boss says you or the people you're working with are stupid or idiots, it's disconcerting. When senior executives use the Lord's name in vain or other foul language, it's awkward. When your boss makes fun of your function in group settings, it's embarrassing and humiliating. When peers, who can't be trusted but are self-serving and motivated by their own political gain, surround you, you find that work can be a very lonely place. What ever happened to treating people with respect, dignity, and honesty? What ever happened to being able to disagree, reach a consensus, and then remind each other that you have a lunch date that day?

The reality is that the evil one sets all this up to tempt you. The evil one wanted me to feel inadequate, lose my confidence and begin to doubt myself, question my abilities, and weaken my resolve to do what is right. There is much to be gained by joining the crowd, be like them, and treat others like they are treating you because it will give you acceptance. In order to keep my position of power, it could have been tempting to act like them, talk about them behind their backs, and place myself in inappropriate situations at bars and other places because it's the politically correct thing to do if you want to fit in.

Treating people like they don't matter is considered normal by people that aren't governed by faith in God. The truth is that God gave me the strength to fight off the evil one and his temptations. He also assured me that he will give me the talents, strengths, and abilities to do my job well in an environment that is not infected by this insidious behavior. He gave me the knowledge to understand that I don't have to remain captive by these people. I had a choice, and my faith got me through it. His love lifted a huge burden by helping me realize that I don't have to work with people who treat others like they do or speak to others like they do to be successful. One day when I had had enough and prayed for the Lord's protection, I realized that if being rich and powerful means I have to be like them, then I would rather be poor and meek.

During this time the Lord gave me a scripture to hold onto which said, "Have I not commanded you? Be strong and courageous. Do not be terrified; do not be discouraged, for the Lord your God is with you wherever you go" (Joshua 1:9.)

Through this scripture in Joshua, which I carry in my wallet, God is saying, "Have I not told you before not to worry? Have I not told you to stand up to them with courage because you are not alone? I am with you always no matter what the day brings and my love for you is everlasting."

Andrew's story is a revealing example of what can happen if people make having success an idol. He found himself working in an environment that was empty of any real meaning because those surrounding him did not really care about people. They cared about succeeding at any cost and making themselves look good even at the expense of others. Not only that, it became obvious to Andrew that in order to succeed with his new boss and fit in with his colleagues, he would have to change his own behavior to fit in—a change that Andrew was not willing to make. Instead he chose to trust that God was with him and would help in any situation. Having continued success was less important to him than staying true to the principles that God had placed in his heart.

If we are to survive having success, we must first know that true success is given by God and is to be used for His glory only. God defines success as doing what He has given us to do to the best of our abilities in the most excellent manner. When we do that, it will result in us receiving many blessings, which could include money, power, and position. But obtaining these things should never be our motivation. Our motivation should always be to serve God and others and to use whatever blessings He provides as a means of glorifying Him. When we have learned to do this, we will have truly gained success.

Chapter Seventeen

Disappointments and Failures

Faith at Work Tip: Failure provides an opportunity to trust God

Beloved, do not think it strange concerning the fiery trial which is to try you, as though some strange thing happened to you; but rejoice to the extent that you partake of Christ's sufferings..." (1 Peter 4:12-13).

After twenty-three years with the firm, Kimberly found herself packing her desk at the office. She couldn't believe it. The day had started like any other day. She had arrived at work as usual and turned on her computer. She returned a few phone calls when she noticed her boss' assistant hovering at her office door. She was being summoned into her office regarding a serious matter. Everything after that point was a blur. Something about an expense report containing false information and the next thing she knew, her twenty-three years with the firm were gone. She had been fired.

No matter what the reason, being fired is tough. Whether it is due to company downsizing, a performance related issue, or jobs being sent offshore, none of us wants to hear the words, "I'm sorry, but you are being terminated." If you've ever been fired, you know the self-doubt this can cause and the second-guessing that can occur. "If only I had..."—fill in the blank and you can instantly recall the feelings that accompany such an event.

Jean is the Human Resource administrator for a local company. Part of her job involves discharging employees from their jobs. The following is her description of it as being one of the most distressing things that she has to do:

No matter what the reason, terminating an individual's employment is never easy because you are profoundly affecting the life of that person and his or her family. Recently, at my office, we went through a staff reorganization when certain positions were eliminated. Thus, it was my job to communicate the termination to a long-time, loyal employee. This staff person was well-loved by the organization, yet there was simply no job to move him into. As I started to explain to him that his job was being eliminated and that there would be no other job for him in the organization, I saw his horror-stricken and shocked face. He had never seen it coming! Tears began to stream down his face. With tears in my own eyes, I told him about the severance benefits, knowing that he couldn't hear me. I grasped for words to say. Suddenly, I said to him, "When God closes one door, He opens another one—I know you will be richly blessed in your next job." All the while I was silently praying a scripture that I had read: "Continue steadfastly in prayer, being watchful in it with thanksgiving; and pray for us also, that God may open to us a door for the word" (Colossians 4:3-4). He finally looked up at me and said in a controlled voice, "Thank you and God bless you." After he left the room, I dissolved into tears—after more than 20 years of terminating people's employment, this was the first time I had cried as a result. I felt that God was saying to me that it was okay to grieve over this man's loss, but God had given me the right words to help the man go on his way. God did indeed open another door for the man; he is in an exciting, new job where he will make a difference in the lives of many.

The loss of a job can be devastating and emotionally can have almost the same impact that the loss of any key relationship can have. For the person of faith, it is no different. We, too, will have the overwhelming feelings that often accompany such an event. How am I going to pay my bills? Who is going to hire me when I don't even have a good resume? What will my family think? If gone unchecked, these feelings of fear can sweep us over the edge if we allow them too.

Our guide, Daniel, also had such an event occur during his career. Daniel began working for his new boss, Darius, after the death of his former boss, Belteshazzar. Daniel and Darius hit it off from the very beginning. Daniel excelled in comparison to his peers, and as a result, it was Darius' intent to promote him to a position above everyone else. As could be expected, Daniel's colleagues were not happy to hear about this promotion and sought a way to block it from occurring. Through some clever finessing, they talked Darius into establishing a work rule that they knew Daniel would be hard pressed not to violate. After getting Darius to implement this new rule, they waited to trip Daniel up so that they could report his violation to Darius. They knew that a violation of this magnitude would result in immediate termination—literally.

They didn't have to wait long. As they had expected, Daniel did in fact violate this new work rule, and gleefully they reported him to the boss. Darius was sick about this turn of events because he really liked Daniel. After all, Daniel was the superstar of his team. But a rule was a rule, and he couldn't make an exception for Daniel. And so Darius had to make a tough decision, he had to terminate Daniel. It is apparent that Darius felt as bad about this decision as my friend Jean did, but like her, he had no other choice.

So how did Daniel handle going from being the company hero to becoming the company pariah? What must he have felt in having performed well for all those years only to have it all taken away in an instant? What must he have thought upon realizing that he was really going to be fired? Since we already know the end of Daniel's story, it would be easy to think that he didn't experience the same emotions that you and I do. But we would be wrong to think so. After all, Daniel was a real person with real challenges in his career and in his life.

Let's start at the beginning. When Daniel first heard about the new rule, he went home. What would cause a person to go home in the middle of a workday? Typically, something major would have to have happened—some event at work that was so disturbing that you believed you needed immediate respite. That's exactly what our friend Daniel was experiencing. He needed time to think about what to do. He knew that the rules had been changed, and he knew that they had been changed in an attempt to get him fired. The bad thing about it was that his enemies' plans were actually working because Daniel knew without a shadow of a doubt that he was going to break the rules. He also knew that there would be consequences to his actions and that is what he needed to think about. That is also what he began to pray about.

If you are familiar with Daniel's story, you may be wondering why God didn't immediately come to Daniel's rescue. Why would God allow him to go through even one sleepless night? After all, Daniel was right not to obey this rule, wasn't he?

The truth is good people do get fired. People of faith get fired. The reasons may vary. It may be through someone's fault, or it may be through no one's fault. It could be for the best business reasons, or it could be for no business reason. It could be that the boss was just out to get you, or it could be that your boss regretfully had to let you go. Whatever the reason, the pain is real, and the devastation of losing one's job is very difficult to take. If there is ever a time when our faith in God's sovereignty becomes challenged, it is when our backs are up against the wall and we think that all is lost. Clearly, getting fired is one of those times.

Whenever, I find myself in a difficult spot, I always ask myself three key questions:

1.   What does God want me to learn about Him through this situation?

2.   What does God want me to learn about me through this situation?

3.   How will this situation bring glory to God and reflect His greatness to others?

Inevitably, when I am able to do this, I am able to remain focused on the right things, the 'God' things. We had an event that occurred in our family that solidified these lessons for me. Many years ago, my husband had been working in a corporate job that he really didn't enjoy. He had always had a dream to own his own business but would never take the risk because he was the primary source of income for our family and felt a great responsibility to me and to our daughter. As a result, he spent many evenings complaining about how much he dreaded his job and really wanted to do something else. Being the sweet thoughtful wife that I was at the time, I responded by telling him to stop complaining and get a grip. I guess secretly I was worried that if he quit his job and started a new business, it might fail, and about where that would have left us.

In the meantime, unbeknownst to either of us, his firm was planning a reduction in force. As it happened, he was one of the many people that received a pink slip. All along, I had been praying for a miracle, but this definitely wasn't it. I couldn't believe it! My husband was actually out of a job. At first, a little panic started to set in. After all, we had financial responsibilities to think about. But then I begin thinking through those three key questions: What does God want us to learn about Him? What does He want us to learn about ourselves? How will this situation bring Him glory and reflect His greatness to others?

You know from your days in school that just because you ask a question, it doesn't necessarily mean that you are going to get an immediate answer or that you will understand the answer if you do. That was my situation. Everyday I would ask, "God what is this all about? What do you want us to know about you during this time? How on earth can you be glorified if your children don't have money to pay their bills or if they starve to death?" (Sometimes, we become dramatic with God, don't we?) While I was attempting to keep panic from setting in, God was behind the scenes working faithfully.

It started when my husband finally decided that this might just be the time to start his own business. After all, he had always wanted to be in business for himself, and we agreed that it wouldn't have occurred to him to simply quit his job to do so. After praying about the decision, we stepped out in faith and he began to pursue his dream of becoming an entrepreneur. That was more than eight years ago, and he has been successfully running his own business ever since.

In that situation, I learned a lot about God. I learned that He is faithful to take care of His children. I learned that He cares about our dreams and our hearts' desires. I learned that even when things seem out of control, He is in perfect control. I learned that He doesn't go about things in the same manner that we do, and that He often takes what appear to be the most bizarre routes to get to the perfect outcome. I learned that He wants us to trust Him and, most importantly, He never fails us. Each of these lessons were important for me to know because there would be days ahead when I would need to be able to rely on the strength of these lessons to get me through other difficult situations.

What did I learn about myself? I learned that my faith was all talk and little action. This experience changed that. I also learned that I had a tendency to want to tell God how to solve things, which was totally unnecessary. Finally, I learned that I had issues involving trust. I thought I had been trusting God, but when push had come to shove, I quaked in my boots. Again, they were important life lessons to learn because my spiritual muscles needed strengthening, and God allowed circumstances to give those muscles a workout.

Finally, how was God glorified and His greatness reflected to others? This is the best part. As a result of my husband losing his job, we have been able to tell everyone that it was the best thing that ever happened to our family. It was the strangest thing—something that could have been devastating completely changed our lives in the most positive ways and ultimately led my husband to a point of complete career fulfillment by his being able to work his dream. Only God can change what could have been a devastating event into a dream come true.

In Daniel's time of crisis, he, too, was reminded again of God's sovereignty, his dependence on God, and God's glory. You see, not only was Daniel fired, but he was thrown into a lion's den full of very hungry lions. Very similarly, whenever one experiences the crisis of being fired, there is usually a period immediately following that can be described only as a time with the lions. It is the time when you could very easily feel as though you are being devoured by your circumstances. Since most of us rely on our jobs to be the primary source of income, the loss of a job can be very threatening, and feelings of fear can be paralyzing.

But you, too, can walk victoriously even if you have lost your job and don't see any jobs looming on the horizon. First, reflect on what occurred and ask God to show you if any of your actions might have caused your current situation. Did you violate any company rules knowingly? Did you neglect to perform your job to the best of your ability? Did you contribute to poor company morale by having a negative attitude? If the answer is "yes," then ask God to forgive you for your part in the matter, and ask Him to help you not repeat mistakes that might have cost you your job. Repentance is very important in gaining a fresh start and beginning again. When we know that we are forgiven, we can approach the job search process knowing that God is for us and He is a God of second chances. On the other hand, if you can honestly say that the circumstances surrounding your termination were not brought about by your actions, but that you are harboring some resentment towards those who you believe have wronged you, then ask God to help you forgive them. Forgiveness is also a very important part of being able to move on. If you allow bitterness to take root, it will be reflected in your future actions and could cost you the opportunity to start fresh with a new firm. People can smell bitterness a mile away, and the last thing you want is to go on a job interview and have that bitterness seep through your conversation with a potential employer.

While going through the process of repentance or forgiveness, begin to ask God what He wants you to know about Him during this time. You can learn this only by spending time with Him and by reading His Word. Ask Him to make it plain to you so that you are confident about His character and His sovereignty. One issue to consider may be your dependence on your job rather than your dependence on God. So often, we forget that our jobs are not our source. Our true source for all things, including our jobs, is God. When we begin to forget that distinction, it is easy to view our jobs as the ultimate source of our financial well-being. While it is true that having a job can be one of our primary sources of income, the fact that you and I may have jobs is because of God's goodness and for no other reason.

Another issue to consider is whether or not you have put your job at a place higher than God is in your life. Sometimes, when we have jobs that we love or have been successful in, we may begin to love our jobs to the detriment of everything else, including family, friends, and particularly, God. We know this to be true when everything else comes second to our jobs. If you spend so much time doing your job that you often have no time for your family, your quiet time with the Lord, or even for yourself, then your job has the wrong place in your life. The loss of it could help you to discover God's desire to be back in His rightful place in your heart and could teach you that having anything in a more exalted place than Him is foolish.

Maybe you have always known that God was your source, and your job never took priority over God or your family, then it could possibly be that God wants you to increase your trust in Him during this time. Whatever God is planning to teach you about Him, you can be assured that it will be useful to you in your life journey and that it is definitely preparing you for the next phase of it.

As you discover more about God, you will also begin to discover more about yourself. What are your feelings about God during this time? Do you have complete confidence that He is in control, or do you find yourself lying awake at night trying to solve the problem yourself? Ask God what He is trying to teach you about yourself. We all have blind spots—areas of our personality that are visible to others but not to us. This is especially true with God. He knows our motives, our secret fears, our dreams for the future, and the desires of our hearts. He knows so much about who we really are, and part of the journey with Him is self-discovery. Have you always viewed yourself as a totally independent person capable of handling anything? You might learn during this time that what you thought was independence was merely bravado. When we begin to know more of who God is, then we can begin to see ourselves more clearly, and with His help, change those things that we need to change.

This brings us to the final question: How can God be glorified through your present circumstances? How does your losing your job matter in the whole scheme of things? Besides increasing our knowledge of God and ourselves, others may come to know Him through the example that we set during this time. Remember when Daniel was in the lion's den? He was unemployed, in danger of being eaten alive, and totally friendless, with no prospects of ever being able to survive his circumstances. But Daniel had prepared himself during his times of prayer for just such a time. He completely and totally trusted that God would bring Him through his circumstances one way or another and waited quietly for God to act.

Imagine the amazement those who were familiar with the situation must have felt when Daniel not only survived and was restored, but he became employed in a better position than he had before. In a very natural sense, everyone had expected him to cave-in under his circumstances, but afterward, they could only marvel at his God. Believe it or not, the same can be said of you as people watch how you handle the loss of your job. If you are a person of faith, now will be the time to walk the talk. Many of your former colleagues and those who know you well will want to see if what you have said about God is true. Does He really take care of His children, and can He be counted on in a pinch? In these circumstances, as well as many others you will face, He will be glorified if you will trust Him to keep His word.

Yes, getting fired is never easy for anyone, but more importantly, it is never too hard for God. After all, He specializes in lion's dens. Just ask Daniel!

PART FOUR

T.G.I.F. (Thank God It's Faith!)

There comes a time in everyone's career where she begins to believe that she's arrived, only to realize that she might have arrived at the top of one hill, but as she gazes out at the horizon, there are many more hills and mountains to climb. It is at this point when we can either become discouraged and see it all as futile or embrace what we've accomplished and look ahead at the next phase of our journey.

I went through an experience like that not too long ago. After spending many years in corporate America, I had achieved the pinnacle of my career goal—to become the national head of a department for a major company. I was delighted! I had worked hard to get there and simply wanted to sit on top of that hill and enjoy it. And, for a period of time, I enjoyed it immensely. I had a great team, a great boss, and the work was interesting and challenging. I loved the company and believed in its mission. But as time passed, I started to look out at the horizon, and I realized there were more hills and mountains up ahead.

I felt confused at first, thinking, *Wait a minute, I've arrived, what's this secret longing I'm beginning to feel to go and explore those other hills and mountains?* And just like that, I realized that I hadn't arrived at all. God was simply calling me out of my comfort zone and requiring that I go higher. It was very scary stuff. After all, I was comfortable, and coming out of a zone that I loved and knew well would take a whole lot of faith. But that is exactly what I did.

It wasn't easy at first. In fact, it was extremely difficult to get motivated to take on what I knew would lie ahead. When you have some experience climbing mountains, you know that there are muscles that you don't use in every day walking. I knew that these muscles were about to be exercised to the maximum, and the Lord knew my tendency to procrastinate when it comes to exercise. But as I continued to practice those strength and conditioning routines that I know so well, such as spending more time in God's Word, having my daily meditation and quiet time, and speaking truthfully those things that God has said about me, my muscle of faith grew larger and larger, tackling those daily giants of doubt and unbelief successfully. And before I knew it, I was moving up those new mountains with confidence, not knowing all the details of how things would turn out, but knowing absolutely that they would turn out well.

In the final chapters of this book, we will explore those times when God calls us higher—past the office politics, over the snares of success, and into a place where the work we do can become an act of worship, honoring God and all that He is in our lives. It is a place where we can declare, "It was nothing but faith in God that sustained me."

Chapter Eighteen

Success, Triumphs, and Promotions

Faith at Work Tip: Success is guaranteed when your motives are pure and your heart is focused on God.

They delight in doing everything the Lord wants; day and night they think about His law. They are like trees planted along the riverbank; their leaves never wither, and in all they do, they prosper...(Psalm 1:3).

Everyone was really happy for Joanna. After the merger, everybody had been scrambling to make sure they had their name in a box on the company's organizational chart, but not Joanna. She was perfectly content to let the chips fall wherever they may. She continued to work diligently, despite the uncertainty of her future, and when she was named for a key position in the organization, everyone was genuinely happy for her. I knew her well and decided to ask her how she had managed to maintain her peace and joy despite all the chaos going on around her.

Joanna reminded me of the events that had led her to this moment. The prior year, Joanna had been diagnosed with a very serious cancer. Being the mother of young children, she had naturally been very concerned about the outcome of her treatment and whether she would survive. She had shared the diagnosis privately with only a handful of co-workers whom she trusted. I had been one of them. During that time, we had stood with her in faith and had interceded on her behalf in prayer. Despite how sick the treatments had made her, she very seldom missed work, and her attitude had always been upbeat and positive. No one would have ever guessed the battle that she had been through.

"Mary, after going through something like what I went through last year, this merger is a cakewalk," she said. I knew that she was right. Her perspective about her job situation was very different from all those around her. She had been through her own lion's den and had come out knowing, above all else, that only God had brought her through triumphantly. As a result, she was completely sure that whatever happened at work, she would be fine and it would all work out for her good. She spent absolutely no time wondering if she would have a job or if she would find success in the newly merged company. Instead, she was thankful for each day that God gave her that was cancer free and thankful that she was well enough to continue to work, despite the unsettling times.

What resulted was that she was assigned to a position that was equal to her previous position and that allowed her to learn some additional skills in an area that she hadn't worked in before. She came through the merger quite successfully. It wasn't so much that she was confident in her past successes and, therefore, knew that she would be selected for a great job. No, instead she projected an attitude of faith in God and demonstrated it by not allowing an uncertain future to keep her from doing the job in front of her. She wasn't getting paid to sit around discussing all of the "what if's," as so many others were doing. She was fully aware that she had had a successful career prior to the merger, but so had others. Instead, her confidence rested solely on the fact that God was more than able to give her favor with the new management team and that if He chose not to do so, she knew it meant He had a better plan in mind for her life.

But what caused her to triumph when so many others in the same situation would have easily lost their way? Instead of facing their futures with confidence, others would have dropped into despair and questioned why it was happening to them—first cancer, now this!

How do we learn to move triumphantly through our circumstances at work and go higher in our walk of faith? Faced with a similar set of circumstances, Daniel, through his response, offers insights into how we can go higher as we live by faith while at work.

Many years had passed since Daniel interpreted the dream of King Nebuchadnezzar. In fact, King Nebuchadnezzar was dead and gone and a new king, totally unfamiliar with Daniel or his past success, was on the throne of Babylon. King Belteshazzar was having a big party and had invited many of his loyal subjects and those important in his kingdom. It is obvious that Daniel was not counted among that number since his name was not mentioned anywhere on the guest list. But there were those in the king's circle who still remembered Daniel by reputation. During the course of the evening, after the king and his noblemen had had too much to drink, a strange thing occurred. Suddenly, a hand appeared and some writing appeared on the wall of the dining hall.

Like Joanna and Daniel, there will be many opportunities for you as a person of faith to go to a higher level in your faith journey at work. The longer that you are in the workforce, the more you will discover the need to take it up a notch. Remember, we are all being made to be more like Christ, and that means that just as you begin to think you've got this faith thing down, you will discover another opportunity to grow in your faith. As wonderful as it is to achieve success at work, it can be a slippery slope, as we have already discussed. Some will begin to idolize their success, and others will become so terrified of losing whatever it was that got them there that they forget why they are there in the first place. As a result, it is important to know how to deal with the success that is God's gift to us. Our attitude in dealing with success will often times be more important than how we deal with failure. We will never be promoted in our faith journey until we have learned how to effectively manage whatever success we have gained at any given point in time. I observed an interesting example of this just the other day.

My husband received the nicest Christmas greeting from one of the postal workers at the post office that he frequents. When I read the greeting and the personal letter that was enclosed, I was fascinated. In it, the postal worker had apologized to him for always being so mean and unfriendly to him and other customers who came into the post office. She said that God had really been dealing with her about her terrible attitude at work. She offered some personal explanations for why she had behaved in this manner, but in the end she just wanted him to know how sorry she was and that she was really working at being a more friendly person in the future.

When I asked my husband to tell me more about this dear lady, he responded by saying, "That lady used to be a scary person to deal with. She was rude and unfriendly. I hated to get in her line, but I always tried to be nice to her, and she was never nice back until recently. For some reason, she has put a little bit of a smile on her face and seems to be warming up some. I didn't know what was going on with her, but I was just glad that she wasn't snapping my head off anymore."

Having read her letter, I believe we can make a few assumptions about what might be going on with this postal worker. God is calling her to go higher. No matter what has caused her to be bitter about her past, she has begun to recognize that she can have a positive impact on her future by changing her approach to her present circumstances. Some might ask, "How is she a success? She's only a postal worker." The truth is that there are many people who would love to have the very job that she was taking for granted. To receive the pay that she is receiving and the benefits that she has been blessed with would be a tremendous blessing to someone who is making minimum wage. In their eyes, she has already achieved a level of success that they are only dreaming of having.

And of course, that is entirely the point. Our achievements may seem small to us or to those around us, but God is in the business of character-building. He is building up people of integrity who treat whatever job they have as one that is as important to Him as if it were the presidency of the United States. If we forget this, then we will never learn to bring glory to God in our everyday triumphs and successes. With that as our perspective, we begin to understand the value of becoming the best "bush" that you can be instead of always wanting to be a "tree."

Is it possible the postal worker lost sight of that in the day to day tediousness of her work? Probably. But I think she is already on the path to changing her future simply by responding to God's leading her to write the letter to her customers, asking for forgiveness and following through by changing her behavior at work. I wish I could be around to see the end of her story, but I have this feeling that if she continues on this path of faith, a promotion is in her future.

Some of our greatest triumphs will come when we decide to go up higher with God. From a career perspective, this might be moving into territory that is unfamiliar to us, such as taking a lateral move instead of wanting to only move upward. How many great opportunities are passed up simply because they are not viewed as promotions? Once we learn that any move we make according to God's plan for our lives is a promotion, we are free to look at our work differently and seek those opportunities that are complementary to the path He has for us.

I love to jog. Some of my best thinking is done while jogging, and I have learned some really interesting life lessons while on a jogging path. One lesson that illustrates the concept of staying focused on God's path for each of us came to me while jogging through the park one day. I was having a fine old time jogging along by myself when I noticed that there was another jogger coming up behind me. Being the competitive creature that I am, I was determined that this jogger was not going to pass me, so I began to pick up my pace. We jogged along for quite some time with me in the lead, but I was becoming more and more tired since I was running at a pace that was past my capacity. But of course, I couldn't give up in shame, so it became a race unto death. With tongue hanging and heart pounding, I ran with all my might and yet it seemed as though my jogging companion was only getting faster, rather than tiring out as I was.

Eventually, this still small voice spoke to my heart and said, "Why are you running someone else's race?" It was a good question. I didn't have a clue. That jogger didn't even know there was a race going on between us, and I didn't know her from Eve, so why was I knocking myself out to beat someone who didn't even know my name? And what did I have to be ashamed of? So what if I couldn't keep up with her? Was the world going to stop revolving around the sun simply because I was losing the imaginary race? Or even if I won it, was I going to receive a key to the city? And with that, I simply slowed down and let her run by.

In our work lives, we do the very same thing. We often begin to run someone else's race for success. We look at how our colleagues define success and decide that their definition applies to us, as well. We already know God defines success differently, but even when we know that, we frequently use a measuring standard that has nothing to do with His definition. Remember, you are successful anytime you are doing what you know God is calling you to do and doing it with excellence. If it happens that in the process you also receive accolades from those with whom you work, it's just added favor and grace.

The way to deal with success when it comes is with great humility and graciousness. This is no place for the fainthearted. Many people of faith have had their heads turned by having more success than they knew what to do with. Before long, we can be in danger of thinking it's all about us, instead of remembering whom we should always seek to glorify. If you find yourself in that place of great success, then you should spend even more time in your prayer closet asking God to keep pride from rearing its ugly head. As happy as God is to bless us with success, we are reminded that it is a great trust that He is also bestowing on us. He is in essence saying, "I can trust you to remember that all good things come from Me."

This doesn't mean that you are required to have a poor self-image or lack confidence in your abilities. It does mean that you recognize that those abilities came from God and ultimately the success you have achieved should be credited to Him. It was God who opened the right doors. He was the one who created relationships that might not have existed before. He gave you favor with the right people, and He gave you the skills and abilities to get the job done. It's hard to take any credit when you see success in its proper perspective. It truly is a "God thing."

Don't fall into the trap of idolizing your success. Enjoy it and glorify God through it, and be thankful that He has entrusted you with it, but hold it lightly. Your job title is not who you are. What you earn does not define you. Even the power you may have as a result of your position at your workplace should not be something that you use only to benefit yourself. If you have been successful, seek first to understand how God might want to use the authority you now have, to help others. What can you do to open doors for those who may need a helping hand? How can you reflect the essence of God's glory through your success?

It is when we use our success to build up others and benefit those around us that we are sharing the love of God. If you've been blessed with success, thank God and then spend time looking for ways that you can bless others in the workplace. We are blessed to be a blessing to others. Success is hollow indeed until it is used to bring glory to the only One who can give it.

Chapter Nineteen

Becoming a Person of Integrity

Faith at Work Tip: Let your behavior at work be an example of who you serve—the Lord

Who is wise and understanding among you? Let him show by good conduct that his works are done in the meekness of wisdom (James 3:13).

I have been working in corporate America for more than 25 years. I can honestly say that I have learned a lot. From my very first job until the position I hold today, I have found there are certain rules that never change in most corporations. Let me give you some examples and see if these sound familiar to you:

- Be nice to everyone, you never know who could end up being your boss.
- Toot your own horn, because nobody else is going to toot it for you.
- Come early and stay late—even if you aren't doing much of anything in between—people seem to be impressed by those colleagues who come early and stay late.
- Develop relationships with as many 'key' people as you can—they may be able to help you in the long run.
- Always CYB!' (This stands for "cover your back.")
- Never let them see you sweat! (my personal favorite)

Welcome to the world of office politics! It is never ending and can be all consuming. Whether you work in a corporation, a school district, church, or other non-profit organization, you will find varying degrees of office politics. It is the grease that makes the entire engine run. But really, it shouldn't be a foreign concept to any of us. After all, haven't we experienced some form of politics since we were all in kindergarten? Haven't we been taught since grade school how to manipulate situations to result in outcomes that were best for us? Then it is easy to understand how the typical workplace continues to breed some of these same behaviors because it is filled with the same type of people with whom we went to school.

Unfortunately, there are simply some things that they don't have a course on in business school. Most of us learned about office politics after stumbling around for years trying to figure out what was really going on around us. I must admit that I was pretty naïve when I first started working. All the people looked like me—two arms, two legs, and one head with a nice smiling face painted on it—so naturally, I thought we were all the same. I quickly learned that we were not. We did have one thing in common—we all wanted to move up in the organization. Other than that, our tactics for getting to the illustrious place known as "ahead" were completely different from one another's. I learned whom I could trust and whom I couldn't trust, but not before I had made a few costly mistakes.

Early on, I made the mistake of confiding in a colleague my thoughts on the substandard performance of another colleague. I was unaware that these two individuals were best friends. Even though my confidant eagerly listened to everything I had to say and even shared a few tasty morsels of her own, she went back and relayed the entire conversation to our mutual colleague and attributed some of her own comments to me. Needless to say, I had just made an enemy, and I wasn't even aware of it. It was though errors in judgment just like that one that I first discovered the difference in merely working and working for God.

You see, when I first began working, I used to check my Christian hat at the door. I don't recall meaning to leave that hat outside, but many of my actions clearly showed that I wasn't applying the Christ-like behavior that I learned on Sundays to the world of work in the office on Mondays. Does that sound familiar? Occasionally, I would fall prey to these errors in judgment while trying to learn the rules of the game. No matter how hard I tried to implement those rules, I begin to have an increasingly difficult time at work. I begin to wonder what was going on. After all, I was coming in early and staying late. I was being nice to those people who could help me, and I was the champion CYB player. So why wasn't it working to my satisfaction?

Since I am an analyst by nature, I begin to analyze my situation. I thought I had the rules down pat, yet something wasn't working, and I didn't feel right either. It was then I decided to go back to basics. All these corporate rules felt insincere to me. In other words, why be nice to someone simply because they might be able to help you? Why not be nice to them because you want to be, or because they happen to be someone that you want to know better, or simply because it makes God happy when we are kind to others?

For me, the basics have always included understanding what God has to say about a matter. Whenever I am perplexed, I make it a practice of saying, "Father, what do you think about this?" Now I must be truthful. Initially, I would make a few stops along the way before asking that question. By that I mean I would first talk to a few girlfriends, or my husband, or maybe a sister or two. But now, I have learned the value of first asking God what He thinks.

As always, God is so willing to teach us when we are open to learning. When I first asked Him for His help in understanding how to work smart in the world of work and how to be savvy in dealing with office politics, He started by showing me how to first work for Him.

Working for God is the beginning of understanding how to avoid office politics. It doesn't mean that you bury your head in the sand and pretend that office politics don't exist. They do, whether you believe it or not. But you have to have incredibly savvy to stay out of the mire and rise above the rest. You have to be disciplined enough to want to avoid a few land mines that will inevitably await you, and you must recognize that as a believer you have a secret weapon: God. He knows the intent and motives of all people. He knows the past, the present, and the future. He knows and understands how we operate and why we do the things we do. Because He knows all this, He is an awesome ally to have in our corner. Or to state it more accurately, it's to our advantage to be in a corner with Him.

Daniel had a great understanding of office politics. Remember, he had to deal with jealous colleagues, a demanding boss, and he had to live in an environment that was totally foreign to him, as well as to learn the office lingo. There is no way he would have achieved his career success or survived some of its obstacles had he not figured out two key-truths that helped him to rise above the politics that constantly surrounded him. What are these truths?

1. God is sovereign.

He is even sovereign at the company or organization where you are working today. You may have the best boss; you may have the worst boss. Your stock may be up; your stock may be down. It doesn't matter what is going on. God is still sovereign. Don't believe for a minute that when you tell God about some of the things going on in your office this week He is saying, "Really? You've got to be kidding! They're doing what?" He is not surprised or shocked because He is still in control even when we are in the midst of difficult circumstances. Are you wondering how you came to find yourself in such a place? Just remember, no matter what the circumstances, God is sovereign, and when we really understand that fact deep within our hearts, our work takes on different meaning and we work differently. We stop playing politics and start focusing on listening to God.

What does that mean, practically speaking? Let's suppose that you do have a boss that isn't on your list of the top 20 people with whom you would want to be stuck on a deserted island. She makes work very difficult. She is demanding, She gives you all the work and takes all the credit. You know the type. If you are still playing office politics, then you may be inclined to figure out some way to sabotage her so that she doesn't look all that good to the folks in the corporate office. Or you may try a different approach and play the game crudely known as "sucking up" in order to manipulate a quick promotion from her. The political games are endless, and some of them might even succeed. But guess what? God is still sovereign. He is completely aware of your circumstances, and He cares about you. This means that you don't have to engage in insincere games or manipulative actions to gain the upper hand. You must simply begin to put into action what you already know by now. You have a higher boss, and He is in charge of the universe.

2. **Office politics is designed for small people, not for those who serve a big God.**

Remember, the reason so many of your co-workers engage in the rampant politics that go on in the office is because most of them believe that they have only themselves to count on. They think the only way to get ahead is to make all the right moves and that it is solely up to them to do all the right maneuvering. I am not implying that it isn't important to be wise and think strategically while at work. However, there is a difference between believing it's all up to you and knowing that God is ordering your steps. When you recognize that you serve a big God, then you stop worrying about what step to take next. You disengage from the political game playing and begin to focus on the bigness of our God.

Remember the story of David and Goliath? When David was still a young teenager, he found himself in what ordinarily would have been an impossible situation. He was to fight a guy who was three times his size and an experienced warrior. He didn't know any of the strategies of warfare, and he had never used any weapons to speak of other than his slingshot. Goliath, on the other hand, had all these attributes, plus he had an incredible ego. He didn't even see David as a real threat and laughed at the thought that David was actually being sent out to fight against him.

Well, you know the end of the story. David not only knocked Goliath down with a rock from his slingshot but also used Goliath's sword to cut off his head. How did David have the wherewithal to implement such a strategy? He knew that the victory wasn't completely up to him. Instead, he was absolutely certain of the bigness of God and trusted Him wholeheartedly for the victory. In the same way, as believers we must be certain that our God is big enough to handle all the office politics that we encounter. We must change our thinking from "It's all up to me" to "It's all up to God." We must seek Him out so that we become as wise as serpents and as harmless as doves.

Being cognizant of these truths, what can we do to remain above the fray of office politics? The first step to rising above office politics is to accept the reality that they exist. Many people bury their heads in the sand and naively think politics are simply not a part of their work environment. You will even hear some say, "I don't engage in office politics," while being able to tell you chapter and verse of all the office intrigues. If your office truly is free from political maneuvering, it is the exception, not the rule. But why is it important for us to know that office politics are a reality? How can that knowledge help us to rise above them? And more importantly, what value is there to rising above them?

We find one reason in Esther's story. Esther was an extremely talented woman, who had been successful in beating out hundreds of other candidates for her job. Esther would have been the first to tell you that it hadn't been easy. The competition was fierce, and every candidate had pulled out all the stops to be recognized and hired for the position. But she had landed the job, was very successful at it, and as a result, became one of the top-ranking officials in the government.

Eventually, there came a time where another high ranking official thought up a scheme to eliminate some of his political enemies. Because of his rank, he had great credibility with the boss and was able to convince him that eliminating these people was in the best interests of their government. Esther was made aware of this scheme and knew that it was wrong because these people were innocent. However, she didn't want to become involved. At first she made all kinds of excuses. It wasn't her problem or her job to be concerned about this issue. Furthermore, who was she to tell the boss what to do? What if she got involved and it made her look bad, or worse, caused her to lose her job? And besides what could she really do to help?

Esther debated all these things in her mind and, at one point, even denied that office politics was at the crux of the matter. She refused to believe that her colleague would stoop so low. Would he really have an entire nation murdered simply because he didn't like them? She finally consulted with her longtime mentor, a wise man, who advised her to take her head out of the sand and start seeing things as they really were. He encouraged her to realize that God had allowed her to beat out all those other candidates for just such an occasion and that she should use her influence to help others less powerful and, thereby, rise above the politics that had started the whole scheme in the first place. And so she did.

Like Esther, as believers, we must accept that politics are all around us. People sometimes engage in behavior that can be unfair and even destructive, all in the name of looking out for number one. Once we accept its existence, it is then that God can use us to rise above it and help those in our circle of influence, as well as teach us to do so with integrity.

Next, if we are truly to rise above office politics, we must be willing to step aside and allow God to lead. Did you ever notice that Daniel never acted just on his own? He always relied on God's leadership and sought His counsel daily. Imagine how different his story would have been if, when his colleagues set him up to get fired, he had tried to figure out a way to get even with them first. He would have missed the miracle of being saved from the lion's den.

Likewise, when we encounter situations that tempt us to engage in office politics and rely on our own strength, we, too, miss the miracles that God wants to demonstrate in our lives. Several years ago, I had a colleague who was known to be very bright and very good at his job. I consulted with him on a number of issues and believed him to be technically sound in his advice. However, he had a manner about him that was quite intimidating to most people because when he believed that he was right, he would shout everybody down until his opinion was the only one in the room that counted.

A day came when he and I didn't agree on an issue and proceeded to get into a heated argument. It reached a point where I had to end the conversation abruptly because I just knew my head was going to explode. Soon afterwards, I started to receive reports that he was talking very badly about me to various important people in the organization. This aggravated me to no end, and I must admit that I was tempted to get even. But I refused to engage in political warfare with him. I determined in my mind that I was going to trust God for justice, and I was not going to speak badly about him or try to defend myself.

Several months passed, and my colleague continued to thrive, or so I thought. Then one day, out of the blue, my colleague's boss called me to tell me that the man was no longer with the organization. I was stunned. Apparently, he had made a really bad error in judgment that resulted in him creating some embarrassment for the firm. As a result, he was fired. His boss went on to tell me that people had begun to complain about him and that it was just a matter of time before they would have had to terminate him anyway. I couldn't believe it! As far as I knew, this guy was untouchable. This turn of events was not coincidental as far as I was concerned. I didn't lift a finger to defend myself or even try to get even with him. All I did was trust that God was in control and then get out of His way so that He could lead me to take the right actions, which in this case meant I had nothing to do but pray. I wasn't praying that my colleague would get fired; I was praying that God would make it known that he was someone who could not be trusted or believed. I saw the miracle of that prayer being answered when I avoided the temptation to engage in office politics, and instead allowed God to lead me.

One of the best ways to rise above office politics is to guard what we say and what we do. We must never say anything about someone or do anything to someone that we wouldn't want revealed on the evening news. If you know that what you are about to say is not something that you would want the person being spoken of to hear, don't say it. If you are about to take some action that would cause others to question whether you are truly a disciple of Christ, stop. Most office warfare begins with gossip, innuendo, and speculation: People talking about people: people putting down others: people taking sides: people spreading rumors; people doing things to outmaneuver someone else. And for what purpose is it done? The majority of the time it is usually to get ahead.

As believers, that is not how we should operate. This does not represent who we are. We are not trying to obtain promotions that don't belong to us. We shouldn't want to talk down others just to make ourselves look good. God's plan for our lives is so much better than that. If we allow Him to, God will promote us in His own time and for His own good purpose. Until then, we must always seek to rise above anything that doesn't bring Him glory, and that includes office politics. Remember, if you are called by His name, then you are called to play by His rules. When you do, you will walk in integrity, and you will never have to be ashamed.

Chapter Twenty

Praying Like Daniel

Faith at Work Tip: God hears all our prayers.

Do not Fear Daniel; for from the first day that you set your heart to understand, and to humble yourself before your God, your words were heard; and I have come because of your words (Daniel 10:12).

One of the most important disciplines that a person of faith can begin in her life is the discipline of prayer. Learning to pray can benefit you personally, professionally and of course spiritually. This is modeled so well throughout Daniel's life, and it has always been the one factor that stood out about his life and his career. In fact, if there were one principle that I learned from Daniel, it would be the importance of having daily prayer time with God. There is no circumstance that he didn't pray about. There was no decision that he made without first consulting God. The intimacy of his prayer life was evident from the moment his story begins and is woven throughout the drama that unfolds throughout the book of Daniel.

As we seek to live our faith at work, our ability to pray effectively will make the difference in how well we do it. Prayer allows us to stay connected to God. It allows us the awesome privilege of entering into His presence and having a conversation with Him. Whether we are there to worship Him, to thank Him, or to make our requests known to Him, we have immediate access to God through our prayers. It is also prayer which provides us with strength to live faithfully at work. When we pray and ask God to equip us to do the work that He has chosen for us, He provides us with the power to do it. Daniel recognized the importance of having a consistent prayer life throughout his life, and he saw the difference it made in his career. He was faithful to pray about matters concerning him and others, giving us an example to follow today. His prayers fell into six specific categories:

- Prayers for God's help (Daniel 2:18)
- Prayers of Praise (Daniel 2:20-23)
- Prayers of Thanksgiving (Daniel 6:10)
- Prayers of Confession (Daniel 9:4)
- Prayers of Intercession (Daniel 9)
- Prayers of Supplication (Daniel 6:11)

It would be realistic to say that Daniel prayed about everything. It was his custom to pray three times a day, which means that he took time during the middle of his workday to pray. It is likely that the two other times took place at the beginning of his day and at the end of it. So it would be safe to imagine that Daniel cast a safety net of prayer around and throughout his entire workday. If we are to pray like Daniel, then we too can enter into a conversation with God about the very same issues that he did. Some of the stories that follow will help you learn how.

Prayer for God's Help

Amy found herself in a tough situation. She had a difficult project to complete, but she wasn't really sure how she was going to get it done. It just seemed as though she was not qualified to do all the analysis that was required on this project. Analysis had never been her strong suit, and she was terrified that her boss would discover that she didn't have the intellectual horsepower to get the job done. She didn't want to fail, but at the same time, she knew that she was in over her head. She begin to remember a verse of scripture that her mother often quoted: "...and those who know your name will put their trust in you, for you O Lord, have not forsaken those who seek you" (Psalm 9:10). She knew that she needed help, and she quietly closed her office door and bowed her head in prayer.

She wasn't sure exactly what to ask God for. And so, she said one simple word, "Help!" and followed that with a quiet, "Amen." She wasn't sure if that qualified as a prayer, but she surely hoped that God had heard her because she desperately needed His help. In the meantime, she continued to work on the project, completing those parts that she could. One day, not very long after she had sent that SOS to God, an intern approached her in the cafeteria at work. The intern had heard about the project that she was working on and was really interested in being a part of it. As they talked about the project, she discovered that the intern was especially good at conducting research and analysis. Amy could barely contain her excitement as she made arrangements for the intern to be assigned to the project. Over the next few weeks, they worked together and learned much from each other. In the end, the project was completed on time and included all the essentials components that were needed to help Amy's boss determine whether they should pursue a particular initiative or not.

Amy learned a lot through that project, but one of the key lessons was about prayer. She learned that prayer is simple, straightforward communication with God about real and immediate issues. Her one word prayer was all that was needed to move the hands of God, and in faith she believes that He provided the intern to assist her to do the work that she needed to do.

Prayer of Praise

As Gwen hung up the phone in her office, she couldn't help but do a little dance beside her desk. She had been working for months to land this account. Her client was not an easy person to deal with, and she knew that there was a lot of competition to gain his business. A few months ago, she had heard that one of her competitors was attempting to underbid her. She knew that there was no way they could provide the service the customer deserved at that price. It was pretty common for her competitor to undercut her price and later not be able to deliver the type service often promised at the time of the deal. She had begun to feel discouraged wondering how long her competitor would be able to get away with this and when someone was going to realize that the guy was all talk.

She had prayed about her presentation and met with the client with confidence. She knew that God wanted her to be a person of integrity and not tell the customer that she could meet that lower bid when she knew that she couldn't. So despite the temptation to do anything to gain his business, she explained to him instead that although her price might be a little more, her service would far exceed his expectations. She proceeded to show him how her company was better than the competition. She walked out of that meeting not being sure if he had been convinced, but knowing that she had done her best.

Weeks had passed before the phone call came through, but finally it had and she was told that she had the account. She danced a jig around her desk and then raised her head up to look at the ceiling just as though she could see the face of God. "Praise you Father for your magnificent integrity. It was only through your example of righteousness that I was able to see clearly how you wanted me to behave in this situation." She continued quietly praising God for His kindness and goodness to her. She knew that she would not always get every account that she worked on, but she always wanted to be able to know that she had modeled God in each business transaction. Her prayer of praise was to simply acknowledge his presence in her life.

Prayer of Thanksgiving

Monica had been working for her company for several years but had seen the opportunities for advancement diminish as the industry continued to consolidate. She had started to believe that she would never see any significant increase in her salary, since the merit increases at her company were becoming smaller and smaller. She believed that she needed a change and began updating her resume. One day, a friend called her to tell her about a new job at one of the hottest companies in the city. This was a company that everyone wanted to work for, and people were being offered a lot of money to come on board. Monica submitted her resume and was called for an interview.

The interview went well, and before long, Monica received an offer of employment. The offer contained a significant salary increase, great benefits, and an opportunity for a twenty-five percent bonus each year. Monica had hit the jackpot, or so she thought. When she begin to pray and thank God for His amazing provision, she couldn't shake the feeling that something wasn't right. It was as though she knew deep down inside that something was missing about this job, but she couldn't put her finger on it. After all, hadn't she asked God to help her discern whether or not this was the right opportunity? Didn't the fact that the company had made a good job offer suggest that God had supplied all her needs? And yet, she came to the conclusion that she should turn down the offer.

A few months after Monica turned down the job, she received a significant promotion. Not only did she receive an increase in salary and a higher bonus potential, but also, by remaining with her company, she was able to retain her tenure and continue building her retirement. What a blessing! While watching the evening news, she saw a very startling report. The company that had made her an offer of employment only months before was declaring bankruptcy and was laying off almost their entire workforce. Monica's first thought was how close she had come to taking that job and possibly losing everything. That night, when she went into her prayer closet, all she could do was thank God for His mercy. She knew that He had protected her from making a huge mistake and had also blessed her with a promotion, thus meeting the desires of her heart. As she reflected on the goodness of God, she breathed a sigh of relief knowing that a verse of scripture that she had memorized so long ago was continuing to prove true: "...The steps of a good man [woman] are directed by the Lord" (Psalm 37:23). She whispered, "thank you God for always directing my steps."

Prayer of Confession

After many months, Pam had to accept the fact that she had been conned. She had run her own business successfully for years and had believed it was time for expansion. When she met Jim, she thought he was an answer to her prayers. Jim had the expertise that she needed to expand her business into an area that was growing. Jim was articulate, knowledgeable, and confident. He seemed to know her industry well and gave her a list of contacts that were quite impressive. She had to admit that it didn't hurt that Jim was very attractive and well dressed too. So she hired him.

That was the beginning of the end. Jim started off like gangbusters, getting out, meeting the customers, and setting up deals. But none of his deals ever came through. To make matters worse, he was spending a ton of the company's money and had nothing to show for it. Whenever she questioned Jim about his spending, he always retorted,

"You have to spend money to make money," and reassured her that the payback was coming soon.

It never came, and by the time Pam realized that she had been conned, the business had sustained thousands of dollars in loss. Pam was sick about it. She was also furious! After she went over the books with her accountant and realized the scam, she fired Jim. Over and over she asked, "How did I get myself into such a mess?" Every time she thought about Jim, she got madder and revenge often crossed her mind. It got to the point that she couldn't sleep because of the anger that she felt towards him. She just knew that she would never be able to forgive Jim for taking advantage of her and her customers.

Finally, Pam had had enough. She was sick and tired of being angry, and she knew that she needed to forgive Jim, not because he deserved her forgiveness, but because she knew that God wanted her to forgive him. Pam always had her quiet times with God during the evening. It was during these times when she was able to really meditate on His Word. Her constant prayer was that God would give her the ability to forgive Jim. She was able to do that after she asked God to first forgive her. She wanted His forgiveness for never consulting Him about hiring Jim in the first place. She didn't recall even asking God's opinion about Jim. She also asked God to forgive her for allowing Jim's attractiveness to cloud her judgment. When she reflected back on that time, she realized there had been warning signals all along about Jim before she hired him, but she had missed them by being more caught up in what was on the outside of the "package," rather than what was inside. And finally, she asked God to forgive her for harboring anger in her hurt for so long and wishing bad things upon Jim. She knew that Jim did not know God, so why would she expect him to treat people as he would want to be treated?

It was amazing! After finishing her prayer of confession, a huge weight seemed to lift from her shoulders. She knew that God was faithful and just to forgive her of all her sins and to cleanse her of all unrighteousness. How could she not forgive Jim, when God had forgiven her so much? And so she did.

Prayer of Intercession

Annette and Megan had known each other for a long time.

Although they worked in different cities, they worked for the same company and had collaborated on various work-related initiatives over the years. A friendship had ensued, and over time, they begin to share their faith and many details of their personal lives. For example, Annette was aware that, although she was single, Megan had been in a romantic relationship with Fred for more than a decade. Annette knew that Megan was desperate for Fred to marry her, but he simply wouldn't commit. Many times when they met for dinner during their business travels, Megan would bemoan the fact that although Fred was such a great guy and he said he loved her, she couldn't get him to agree to marry.

As a result, Annette decided that she would intercede in prayer for Megan and Fred's relationship. Secretly, she suspected that Fred would never commit to marriage because he was receiving all the privileges of marriage from Megan, without having to marry her. As her grandmother had often admonished her, "Why buy the cow when you can get the milk for free?" Although she knew her friend would not appreciate being compared to a cow, Annette also knew that her situation could be accurately described in that way. She also knew that even though Megan was a person of faith, she clearly did not see that her behavior in the relationship was inconsistent with the teachings of the Bible.

In her prayers for Megan, Annette asked God to enlighten Megan on the true nature of Fred's character and to give her a clear understanding of His will for her life. Annette was faithful to pray for Megan weekly, always mentioning her to God in prayer whenever she came to mind. It wasn't long before Megan called Annette one day at work and told her it was over with Fred. She had come to realize that he was never going to marry her, and she had decided that she no longer wanted to marry him. She also told Annette that she had come to understand the relationship and the way she and Fred had been conducting it had been wrong. She realized that she had a lot to learn before she could enter into another relationship with a man, and she wanted God to teach her to do it His way.

Annette's prayers of intercession for her friend and co-worker had a significant impact on her life. Without Megan even being aware of it, Annette had petitioned God on her behalf. She believed that God was listening to her prayers and felt that He might have even placed her in

Megan's life so that she would have a co-worker who was not only a friend, but a prayer warrior. Throughout her career, Annette would pray for many of her colleagues because she had learned early on the importance of intercession.

Prayer of Supplication

When I began writing this book, I was in the middle of a career crisis. I couldn't decide whether I wanted to stay in Babylon—corporate America—or do something else. I had become disillusioned with the whole corporate scene. The game playing, the budget challenges, the constant changes in leadership and the daily grind were really starting to get to me. I guess you could say I was becoming burned out.

This is not an uncommon phenomenon for anyone who has worked as long as I have. I'm sure it's also a part of middle-age life. It's that time when you step back and say, "What do I want to do for the next half of my life?" Only in my case, I was posing the question directly to God and asking for His direction and guidance for this season of my life. Since one of my life scriptures is Jeremiah 29:11, which basically says that God has a good plan for my life, I wanted to be sure I was staying focused and truly being attentive to God's plans for me.

My prayers during that time were prayers of supplication—honest and humble requests made to a loving God who I knew cared about me. Like Daniel, I have purposed in my heart to follow hard after God. I want my professional career to always be pleasing to Him, and I want to remain anywhere He places me for as long as He wants me there because I believe my ministry is to serve in that place. Therefore, my prayers during that time were fervent and transparent: "God am I where you want me to be? Is this stirring in my heart an indication that something is about to change? I need to know with certainty, Father, what it is You want me to do. Give me a peace about the future and my place of service." They were quiet, humble prayer requests, made in faith, with the expectancy that an answer was on the way. This was one of the greatest lessons I learned from Daniel: the discipline of prayer and the importance of staying connected to God everyday in every season of life.

No matter where you are in your career journey—just entering the job market, a seasoned veteran, or making plans for retirement—always remember the lessons from Daniel and the importance of staying connected to God through prayer. Prayer moves the hands that rule the world. When we honestly seek Him, we will find Him. And believe me, you need to know that when you are living by faith nine to five.

Chapter Twenty-One

No Hint of Smoke

Faith at Work Tip: Take one day at a time, always looking to God for guidance for that day.

You must accept whatever situation the Lord has put you in, and continue on as you were when God first called you (1 Corinthians 7:17).

Would you change the way you work today if you knew for certain that every word and thought would be examined by God ? Think about it as you go about your work today. Actually think about what you're thinking about and determine for yourself whether your thoughts and words would pass the test. Our actions are preceded by our thoughts. If our thoughts are God-approved, then the words and actions that follow them will be sanctioned by Him as well.

One key attribute that we can take from Daniel's life is the thought-fulness of it. We already can see that he was a man with a committed prayer life, but in reading between the lines, we also observe him thinking about what he was thinking about. He always seemed to be asking, "What does God think, and how do my thoughts reflect His?" As a result, his attitude and his actions were consistent with his prayer and thought life.

It takes work to live by faith in the office. It sounds redundant, but it is true. The life you have chosen as a person of faith will have its ups and downs. The day to day dramas at work or even the tediousness of it can sap the average person of all energy. The high points in your career can be just as taxing as the low points. Whether good or bad, stress is still stress, and learning to go through your days victoriously doesn't simply happen. It requires a person of determination who is willing to spend the time needed in prayer to gain direction, and who has a determined heart to live her faith at work. Is that who you are? If not, is it the person you are determined to become?

Anne asked herself that very question. As a person of faith who had been on the job for several years, she realized that she had compromised in some areas of her work life. From all outward appearances, Anne was a diligent worker, a model employee. However, there were times when she had allowed herself to get caught up in a lot of the office politics. She didn't always support her boss and sometimes allowed it to affect her attitude. And to be honest, even though she knew gossiping was wrong, she had a tendency to be all ears when the latest office rumors started. Although generally a hard working person, she knew there had been days when she had not given her best effort. Instead of working on a report that was due, she had taken a slight detour to play solitaire on her office computer instead. She had justified it by saying, "Everyone was doing it," and after all, if the company didn't want her playing computer games, why did they load the software on her desktop? Or when she was supposed to be participating in a conference call, she often placed the phone on mute so that she could still watch Oprah from the small TV that she kept on her shelf in the office. She knew she had developed some bad habits. The fascinating part about it was that her employer thought she was doing a great job. Her reviews were always good, and she typically received pay increases. However, it didn't change the fact that she knew, and more importantly God knew, that she was compromising.

This weighed heavily on her mind for many months. She often wondered how many of her co-workers were making judgments about who she was as a person of faith, based on her actions. It got to the point where she couldn't even enjoy Oprah anymore because her sense of guilt was growing every day. Finally, she had had enough. She knew that she needed to go up higher with God. She didn't want to settle for a mediocre work life. She wanted to set the standard, rather than barely meeting it. From that day on, she determined in her heart that she would work differently. And she did.

Anne's work life may resemble many of ours. She wasn't doing anything that the normal, average person hasn't been known to do at some point or another. What made the difference was that she became aware of how average she was becoming despite the fact that, as a person of faith, she had been called to a higher standard. Once she became aware of the areas in which she had begun to compromise, she had a desire to change them. She wanted to go to the next level in her spiritual journey and was determined to be a better example at her place of work.

As with Anne, you may find yourself in a quandary about areas at work where you have compromised by having a mediocre standard. One of my favorite things about God is that He is one who gives second chances, again and again. We always have new mercy from Him everyday. As we become aware of those things that we believe may not be God's best for us, we have the ability to start afresh. The story of Daniel is a model of who each of us can be in our places of employment. We may not always be as successful as he seemed to have been at getting it right the first time, but like him, we serve an awesome God who is in our corner and wants us to succeed.

As a person of faith, you are God's ambassador in the place where you work. During the best of times and the worst of times, you are still the one He has chosen to represent Him in that place. You have the greatest opportunity to give others a glimpse of who He is in your life by your words and actions. Some may never set foot in a place of worship but could be moved to desiring a closer relationship with Him by your example of faith. That is why you have been placed there. It is a great responsibility. But with God's help, you are more than qualified to do the job. If you are like me, you have always wanted to live a life with purpose. Well guess what? You can!

Here are a few final thoughts as you begin anew today:

1.   Have a consistent quiet time planned for each day—a time that allows you to communicate with God in prayer, to meditate on His words, and to listen to His voice for direction. Make this your greatest priority ahead of anything else you have planned for that day. Don't become caught up with the duration of your quiet time. On some days, you will have more time than on others. During some seasons of your life, you will have less time than during others. No matter what, spend

some time quietly with God every day. In order to be the best ambassador you can be, you must have this time alone with Him. Use your commute time while traveling to work whenever possible if things become too hectic, or your lunch break. He is a great lunch companion. Of course, if you can, set this time early in the morning before you start your day because it's wonderful to have your marching orders before you leave for work. But even if morning is not your best time, don't let this deter you from setting a time with Him. If you set aside the time with Him, I guarantee He won't be late.

2.   Learn to spend part of your day in worship. There are so many reasons to worship God. The mere fact that He is God is reason enough to give Him praise. But when we enter a time of worship, it reminds us (not Him) of who He is. It reminds us of how much greater He is than our circumstances. It reminds us of His mighty nature and His unmatched accomplishments. It reminds us that He is altogether wonderful, and that He is love. It reminds us of His compassion, His mercy, and His love for us. Because it reminds us of all these things and more, we leave the experience of worship rejuvenated, revitalized, and empowered to do those things He has placed in our hearts to do. Worship changes our perspective. Instead of focusing on ourselves and our limitations, it forces us to focus on Him and the infinite nature of who He is.

3.   Don't allow the past or the mistakes made in it to stop you from embracing your future. Just think what would have happened if Moses had allowed his act of murder to stop him from pursuing God's purpose for his life? Or what about King David? He took another man's wife and then had him murdered to hide the affair, yet he still was known as a man after God's heart. Peter could have allowed his denial of Christ to ruin his entire future, but instead, he confessed the sins of his past and started again with the determination to pursue the purpose that God had for him. And who can forget Paul, the greatest persecutor of the church who ever lived. He allowed God to take his misguided life and use it to become one of the greatest evangelists of the new church. These are only a few examples of how others overcame their past mistakes and still were used in the place where God put them

to make a difference in the lives of others. The same is true of you and me. Our past mistakes are not too bad for God to still use our lives. In fact, they allow us to know for sure who is really at work when we see what we can become through Him.

4. See your work as an opportunity for ministry. Many times we make the mistake of thinking that because we are in a secular job, we are not in ministry. Nothing could be further from the truth. While being able to be in full-time Christian ministry might be the plan for some, it is not where we are all meant to be. However, we are all to go into every person's world and declare the good news of the Gospel. Your place of employment may be one of those places that gives you the opportunity to fulfill this great commission. Although your challenge will be to minister in a way that doesn't interfere with your primary purpose while at work—which is to do the work you are being paid to do—you will be amazed by the ministry you will have as a result of looking for the ways that God wants to use you in the lives of others.

As a person of faith, you will find that this can be the most re-warding type of ministry if you remain sensitive to God and the way He directs your actions. Wherever He has sent you, He also equipped you to go. Everything you need to succeed in God's plan, you already have. Remember when Daniel and his friends first arrived in Babylon? They already had the talent, the ability, and the intellect to learn the things necessary for them to be successful in their new jobs. Throughout their long careers, that fact never changed. As they remained faithful to stay abreast of changes going on around them and always stayed true to their faith, they continued to succeed in the place that God had planted them.

You may need to discipline yourself to look for God's provision in your own life and to properly use it, but it's there. There will be days when you will find yourself in the lion's den, and there will be other days when you will believe you have just been thrown into a fiery fur-nace or two. But like Daniel, you can come out of these experiences with no teeth marks and no hint of smoke because you are following a faithful God who cares about His people. You are never alone. He is with you in the middle of all your circumstances, and there is no circumstance too great for Him. There will be days when it will be hard to remember that as you continue your journey. But the just shall live by faith, and that includes while we are working nine to five.

APPENDIX

Prayers for the Workplace

Faith at Work Tip: Praying for others is an excellent way to share God's love

Therefore submit yourselves to every ordinance of man for the Lord's sake, whether to the king as supreme, or to governors, as to those who are sent by him for the punishment of evildoers and for the praise of those who do good. For this is the will of God...(1 Peter 2:13-15).

As we have learned, one of the reasons Daniel was so successful in his career was his habit of prayer. While we are not privy to all the prayers that he must have said in his lifetime, we can almost be certain that they included prayers for his place of work. The Bible says that the prayers of a righteous person are very effective. Why? Because God listens to us when we pray, and when we pray according to His will, amazing things begin to happen!

This section includes some prayers for the workplace. We are encouraged to pray for others, but sometimes it's hard to get started. These prayers can help you get started, but they should not take the place of the specific issues that you may want to address with God through prayer each day. After all, God is our heavenly Father, and He loves to hear the thoughts of our hearts, not because He doesn't know what we are thinking, but because He enjoys spending time with us and helping us with the problems that are a part of daily living. Prayer is for our sakes so that we form the habit of constantly communicating with God.

I would encourage you to pray daily for your employer, your co-workers, and all of those who you come in contact with at work. Form a habit of writing down some of your specific work-related prayer requests and enjoy looking back to see how God answers your prayers. Over a period of time, you will begin to notice a pattern: God is faithful to answer all our prayers. His answers may not be exactly what we had expected, but His answers will be the perfect solutions.

Prayer for Your Company

Thank you, Father, for allowing me to work at this firm. I know that while I am here, I have a marvelous opportunity to share Your love, grace, and compassion with those I encounter each day. Help me to be faithful in demonstrating Your mercy and kindness so that others will be compelled to seek You due to the example I set at work. Father, I know that as Your child, everything I touch will prosper. I ask the same thing for this company. Let this company be a beacon of integrity in the communities it serves. Let the product we produce or the service we provide be recognized as the best in our industry. So many people depend on this company, Lord, as a means to meet their financial needs, to be productive, and to make a difference in their professions. Because of this, Father, I ask that You will bless this company with customers and clients. I pray that You will give us creative ideas to improve the quality of our products or services. I pray that You will show us how to execute our strategies flawlessly, and that You will cause our business to grow and expand. Father, I know that You care about work and that You were the first employer back in the Garden of Eden. Help my employer follow the example You set by setting expectations and establishing fair consequences when those expectations are not met. But also let them always remember to reward all of those who do meet the expectations and assist in the company's profitability. Lord, I declare that this company will be a great place to work and that everyone who walks through its doors will sense, without even knowing why, that the Spirit of the Most High God is here. Amen.

Prayer for Your Leaders

Thank you, Father, for the people you have placed in charge of my company. I specifically pray for our board of directors, our CEO (insert CEO's name), and our senior management team. Lord, they have a big job to do, and the decisions they make affect the lives of many. Help them to execute their duties justly. Give them wisdom to know in which direction to take our firm. Let them be people of integrity and honesty. Let them always treat the employees and customers of the company as they would like to be treated. Surround them with hard-working, motivated people who can help them realize the mission and vision of our firm.

Father, I also pray for my boss (insert boss' name). I know that only you can give power and authority. You have given my boss authority over me. Help me to respect my boss's position of authority. Let me never be guilty of speaking negatively about my boss to others or of intentionally sabotaging what my boss is trying to accomplish. Help me to go out of my way to serve my boss as though I were serving You—because I would be serving You. Lord I pray that You will bless my boss and cause (insert name) to succeed in the work that she has to do. I declare that I will have favor with my boss and that we will develop a strong working relationship. But most importantly, dear Father, I pray that if my boss does not know You, that You will introduce Yourself promptly and that (insert boss' name) will come to a saving knowledge of You and become Your friend. Amen.

Prayer for Your Co-Workers

Dear Father, thank You for the people that I work with each day. My co-workers have been a source of inspiration for me and have also been a source of agitation for me, but I know that each one of them has been placed in my life for a purpose. Lord, help me to see that purpose. Help me to be "Your person" in this place. Let them see Your presence in me through my actions, words, and deeds. Give my co-workers wisdom and knowledge to do their jobs well. Help them to remain productive and not to get caught up in petty jealousies and rivalries.

Help them to avoid gossiping about each other or doing manipulative things to get ahead at the expense of others. Help all of us to see who is really behind that behavior and learn to resist it. Lord I declare Your favor and blessings in the lives of my co-workers. I ask that You specifically bless (insert the names of your co-workers). Cause them to have peace in their lives and joy in each day. Lord, if they do not have a personal relationship with You, I ask that You would draw them to Yourself so that they, too, might enjoy Your splendid friendship. You know each of their needs much better than I do, Father, so I ask that You would meet their needs and help them to do their jobs to the best of their ability.

Father, today I declare that my co-workers are blessed and that my relationship with each of them will be strong and fruitful. Please eliminate any strife, bad attitudes, or negative spirit that would come to disrupt the harmony that we so desire here at work. You are a God of mercy, and I ask for Your mercy on behalf of my co-workers today. Amen.

Prayer for Your Staff

Thank you, Father, for giving me a great team to work with. You have made me responsible for each of these employees, and I do not take that responsibility lightly. Lord, I ask that You would show me how to effectively lead this team. Direct me in Your ways, Father. Teach me to be a just, fair, and compassionate leader who really cares about the lives of the employees whom You have entrusted to me. Help each member of my staff to be committed to do the work that has been given to them. Help them to be creative and productive. Help them to always consider the needs of our customers and to work collaboratively with one another to accomplish the goals of our work unit. Help them to form friendships with each other and to look for ways to assist each other in getting the work done. Lord, let no strife exist between them, but instead, let there be a spirit of collaboration, respect, and humility.

Give us a true team spirit, allowing us to put the needs of our clients above any selfish ambitions or selfish motives. Help us to meet our work goals and contribute to the mission of our workplace. I pray blessings on each member of my staff. I ask that through my actions and my words, my staff will be able to see the light that only You can bring. Specifically, I pray that if there be any member of my staff who does not know You, Lord, then You would draw them to You. Give me appropriate opportunities to tell them about You whenever possible. However, Father, in those times when it may not be appropriate, let me be sensitive to the leading of Your spirit. Let my actions demonstrate Your loving-kindness in everything I do. I ask all these things in Your name. Amen.

Prayer for Your Clients/Customers

Father, thank You for the privilege of serving others. You have given me these customers, and I know that they are a blessing to me. Help me to be a blessing to them as well. Help me to serve them faithfully and to really listen to their concerns. When they have a problem with a product that I provide or a service that I deliver, give me wisdom to know exactly how to fix it. Lord, I know that You are the source of all my needs. I ask You to continue to give me new clients as I faithfully demonstrate my willingness to serve my current ones. Expand my borders, Lord, and allow my business to grow. When I meet with a new client, help me to discern their needs and think of creative ways to meet those needs. Let customers be drawn to my place of business and want to do business with me. Let me receive referrals, Lord, from sources that I am not even aware of and allow my business to have a good reputation as I seek to honor You in all my transactions.

Father, I declare that my clients are blessed. I speak words of blessing over them each day as they go about their daily business. Even when they are bad-tempered Lord, I will not take it personally, but will instead seek to understand their frustration and to demonstrate mercy by continuing to serve them faithfully. I know that when I serve them, I am ultimately serving You, and I count that a privilege. Don't allow me to lose sight of that, Father, when I go through difficult days serving my customers. Instead, let me serve them with joy and allow them to feel Your presence through me. Thank You for each of my customers, Father. I am simply delighted that You chose for me to serve them. Amen.

Prayer for Your Vendors/Service Providers

Lord, I am so thankful for the people You have sent to help me as I help others. Each of these service providers has a unique talent and is equipped to assist me in being more productive. I am amazed by the abilities that You have placed in each of them, and I ask that You show me the best way to utilize their unique gifts.

Lord, as these people serve me, help me to serve them, as well. Let my attitude toward them be gracious and accommodating, not condescending or mean-spirited. Remind me to treat them as I would like to be treated. Help me to give them clear directions and to establish my expectations up front. Help me to be fair with them when things don't go exactly as planned or if they don't provide the service that they committed to. Let me forgive them for mistakes that they make and be reminded that I am not perfect either. At the same time, teach me to hold them accountable for providing the service that they have agreed to provide and the strength to address those issues that are inconsistent with our work agreement.

Father, I declare that my vendors are blessed. I ask You to bless their businesses and their products. Let them be people of integrity. Let them always choose the right paths of honesty and fair-dealing. Help them not to be tempted to cut corners or take unfair advantage of their clients but to always seek to do the very best job of serving their customers, including me. God, You are more than able to help me discern which vendors I should do business with. Let me discern that now, and let me always choose those vendors who are serving You. Amen

Prayer for Your Job

Father, I enter into Your courts with thanksgiving and Your gates with praise. I declare, Father, that this is the day that You have made, and I will rejoice and be exceedingly glad in it. Father, I thank You for this position that You have blessed me with here at my job. I do not take it for granted, but instead, I commit to performing for You, and not man, in every task assigned to me. I will show myself a faithful steward over what You have given me, and in return, Your blessings shall abound in my life, for Your Word says that a faithful person shall abound in blessings.

Give me the strength, Lord, and move in me throughout this day, regardless of circumstances or situations. Help me to operate in the fruit of the Spirit at all times. That means that even when I feel like losing control of my tongue—whether it is to speak forth gossip, to curse man, or anything that is considered corrupt communication—I won't, because Your Spirit abounds in me and You said, "I am the light," and to let my light so shine. I choose to let my light shine, and as a result, I'll only speak words that bring edification to You and others, and I'll not participate in anything that does not edify others or me. Thank you, Father, for being the Messiah in my life, my banner, my shield, and my strong tower. You are the One who fights all of my battles; therefore, I don't have to. Instead of trying to handle difficult situations or people myself, I'll turn them over to You, Lord, and You will work it out for me because You care that much for me. Thank you, Father, for being all that You are to me. I will never find anyone who will be as good to me as You are. I love You. Amen.

ABOUT THE AUTHOR

Mary E. Banks is the founder of W. O.W. Consulting Group, a firm formed with a specific focus on providing life coaching for women in leadership. Her practice has since expanded to include human resources consulting, strategic planning, team building, and conflict resolution in the workplace. Formerly a human resources executive in the financial services industry for over twenty years, Mary's passion is encouraging the hearts of her clients and empowering them to realize the divine plan and purpose for their lives. She is a sought after keynote speaker, teacher and workshop facilitator as well as the author of The Multi-Faceted Woman. She and her husband, Melvin, and their daughter live in Houston, Texas.

A Dynamic Speaker for All Occasions!
Conference Key Note, Training Workshops, & Coaching!
Mary is an expert with experience in Team Building,
Leadership Development, Life Coaching, and Change Management

To contact Mary for consultations
or speaking engagements, e-mail:

Mary Banks
W.O.W. Consulting Group
Mary_Banks@wowconsultinggroup.com
More information is available at www.wowconsultinggroup.com
or phone: 281.537.5959